AMERICA'S
ANCIENT CITIES

By Gene S. Stuart   Photographed by Richard Alexander Cooke III

Paintings by H. Tom Hall

Prepared by the Special Publications Division
National Geographic Society, Washington, D.C.

Contents

Storm clouds billow above platform mounds at Moundville, Alabama. PRECEDING PAGES: *Temple-pyramids loom beyond a bustling market in the Aztec capital of Tenochtitlan.* PAGE 1: *Traditional hairstyle and dress enhance the classic Maya profile of Maria Cach Cabrera of Ticul, Yucatan.*

HARDCOVER: EMBLEM GLYPH OF THE MAYA CITY OF COPAN
IN HONDURAS; ART BY BARBARA W. FASH

AMERICA'S ANCIENT CITIES

By GENE S. STUART
Photographed by RICHARD ALEXANDER COOKE III
Paintings by H. TOM HALL

Published by THE NATIONAL GEOGRAPHIC SOCIETY
GILBERT M. GROSVENOR, *President and
Chairman of the Board*
MELVIN M. PAYNE, THOMAS W. McKNEW,
Chairmen Emeritus
OWEN R. ANDERSON, *Executive Vice President*
ROBERT L. BREEDEN, *Senior Vice President,
Publications and Educational Media*

Prepared by THE SPECIAL PUBLICATIONS DIVISION
DONALD J. CRUMP, *Director*
PHILIP B. SILCOTT, *Associate Director*
BONNIE S. LAWRENCE, *Assistant Director*

Staff for this Book
MARGERY G. DUNN, *Managing Editor*
THOMAS B. POWELL III, *Illustrations Editor*
VIVIANE Y. SILVERMAN, *Art Director*
VICTORIA COOPER, PATRICIA F. FRAKES,
Researchers
BARBARA A. PAYNE, JEFFREY A. SCHLOSBERG,
Research Assistants
RICHARD M. CRUM, ALICE JABLONSKY,
TOM MELHAM, H. ROBERT MORRISON,
Picture Legend Writers
JUDITH F. BELL, *Map Editor*
ROSAMUND GARNER, *Editorial Assistant*
ARTEMIS S. LAMPATHAKIS, *Illustrations Assistant*
MARISA J. FARABELLI, *Art Secretary*
JODY BOLT, *Consulting Art Director*

Engraving, Printing, and Product Manufacture
GEORGE V. WHITE, *Manager*
VINCENT P. RYAN, *Assistant Manager*
DAVID V. SHOWERS, *Production Manager*
GEORGE J. ZELLER, JR., *Senior Assistant
Production Manager*
LEWIS R. BASSFORD, *Assistant Production Manager*
TIMOTHY H. EWING, *Production Assistant*
CAROL R. CURTIS, *Senior Production Staff Assistant*

SUSAN A. BENDER, BETSY ELLISON,
KAYLENE KAHLER, SANDRA F. LOTTERMAN,
ELIZA C. MORTON, *Staff Assistants*
BRYAN K. KNEDLER, *Indexer*

Library of Congress CIP Data: page 196

Foreword

by Jeremy A. Sabloff

University Professor
  of Anthropology and
  the History and
  Philosophy of Science
University of Pittsburgh

The rise of settled villages and the later growth of towns and cities were two of the most important developments in human history. They are of enduring interest to scholars in many fields, and they provide the focus for this book.

America's Ancient Cities presents an illuminating account of current archaeological views on a variety of permanent settlements in pre-Columbian North America—from small villages in Alaska to major urban centers in Mesoamerica. New discoveries at such sites as Copan in Honduras and Cahokia in Illinois are as astonishing to us in their way as the magnificent Aztec capital of Tenochtitlan was to the Spaniards. But instead of wondering whether to believe our eyes, we are gaining fuller and clearer pictures of ancient cities from careful field excavations and highly technical laboratory analyses.

Archaeology and allied disciplines are beginning to give us new information about how the great centers of the past grew and functioned. This knowledge will surely help correct many of the biases that color current thinking about cities, and should help widen our view of what cities are—not only skyscraper-dominated places with automobile-clogged streets, but also less imposing locales which nevertheless have high population den-

6

sities and complex economic, political, and religious activities.

Ancient peoples in urban settings grappled with a number of vexing questions, many of which have a very modern ring. Recent archaeological studies have shown that they had to cope with problems of overpopulation, depletion of resources, misuse of the environment, and urban renewal. The organization of manufacturing, the growth of service industries, and the efficient movement of goods—these, too, were important concerns.

My own research on urbanism has led me to believe that if we can understand the problems which the development of cities helped solve—and the new ones they created—then we will be in a position to examine productively our own urban problems. And if we can comprehend the successes and failures of ancient cities, then we can profit from that knowledge in attempting to plan future urban growth. Archaeology cannot provide solutions to present-day issues, but it can offer new perspectives.

As familiar as I am with many of the sites featured in this book, I still found myself amazed by the beauty of the photographs and paintings that accompany the clear, informative, and stimulating text. I am sure that readers will enjoy the pages that follow as much as I have. ∎

PROLOGUE

"And when we saw all those cities and villages built in the water, and other great towns on dry land, and that straight and level causeway leading to Mexico, we were astounded. These great towns and *cues* [pyramids] and buildings rising from the water, all made of stone, seemed like an enchanted vision. . . . Indeed, some of our soldiers asked whether it was not all a dream. . . . this first glimpse of things never heard of, seen or dreamed of before."

So wrote Bernal Díaz del Castillo, a soldier in the army of Hernán Cortés, as he recalled the first view the Spaniards had of Tenochtitlan, capital of the Aztec empire. It was November 1519. As guests of the emperor, known today as Moctezuma II, Cortés and his troops toured the capital and, accustomed to the stench and grime of Old World cities, marveled at its glistening cleanliness.

Cortés described the city's splendors in a letter to his emperor, Charles V. He wrote of visiting one market square "twice as big as that of Salamanca, with arcades all around, where more than sixty thousand people come each day to buy and sell. . . ." Soaring temples were "so well constructed in both their stone and woodwork that there can be none better in any place. . . ." Elite dwellings flanked wide avenues and canals. "All these houses have very large and very good rooms and also very pleasant gardens of various sorts of flowers both on the upper and lower floors." City organization, too, impressed the Spaniards—there were judges, priests, and a hierarchy of warriors. Urban amenities amazed them—there were libraries, even zoos.

Moctezuma ruled the largest, most sophisticated city in North America at that time. It housed as many as 200,000 people and administered an empire that included perhaps six million souls. Cortés conquered Tenochtitlan, then razed and rebuilt it as the Spanish colonial capital called Mexico City. Experts predict that the sprawling modern metropolis that grew from those ancient roots will become the largest city in the world, with as many as 30 million people by the year 2000.

What is a city? Broadly defined, it is a large settlement

Aztec soldier made of clay stands poised as if for battle. Wings, talons, and beak helmet identify the figure as an eagle warrior. The Aztecs forged an empire in Mesoamerica in the 15th and 16th centuries.

C. 5½ FEET HIGH, MUSEO NACIONAL DE ANTROPOLOGÍA, MEXICO CITY

FOLLOWING PAGES: Under northern lights, Ice Age hunters on the Bering land bridge return to camp with a speared caribou. Others carve and cook meat from an earlier kill; hides provide clothing and shelter. Pursuing large game, nomads wandered from Asia into present-day Alaska perhaps 14,000 years ago.

with a dense population that includes a variety of specialized people working in nonagricultural professions. A city can be a seat of political power, religion, or trade and industry; often it includes all of these in varying degrees. Cities are a recent development in the story of mankind and a major step in the social evolution that is still occurring.

For 99 percent of human history, people throughout the world lived in temporary hunting camps or, at most, small villages. Only the rise of agriculture allowed people to produce food from permanent sources rather than depend upon hunting wild animals and gathering wild plants. In the early stages of agriculture, settlements were usually small and impermanent, for low productivity required each band of related families to have the option of perennial migration.

The great technological innovation of efficient farming allowed the world's first small permanent settlements to develop. These villages gave people mutual aid and protection and an efficient means of exchanging goods. Often, one or two villages in a given area would expand into centers of trade and production. (Towns are sometimes difficult to distinguish from large villages, just as small cities are often virtually the same as large towns.)

Around 3500 B.C. the world's first cities evolved from agricultural villages and towns in Mesopotamia. Soon afterward cities also developed in other rich agricultural areas of the East—

Shimmering channels meander seaward near Cape Krusenstern, Alaska. Farther south, along the Alaska Peninsula, gulls sweep the sky (opposite) above Afognak Island. By around A.D. 1400, ancestors of today's Eskimos had settled Alaska's southern frontier.

Egypt, then India. By 1500 B.C. the Yellow River region in China supported urban life. All these early cities had centralized governments controlled by elites, with commerce, legal systems, and writing systems. Standing armies protected them. Cultivated fields fed them. Taxes or tribute helped maintain them. Usually they were centers of large political areas called states.

Despite similarities, villages, towns, and cities in the Old World and the New developed in distinctly different ways. North American cultures had no beasts of burden, nor did they have sails. Ancient wheeled toys from Mesoamerica show that some cultures there had knowledge of the wheel, but no practical use for it. Everything from harvested crops to building stones moved by human power. Only the Maya culture attained fully developed writing, although others did have less sophisticated hieroglyphic systems. Metals were used almost entirely for ritual paraphernalia or exotic objects such as jewelry for the elite. For all practical purposes, North Americans remained Stone Age peoples until European contact, and scholars believe their cultures developed in isolation from those of the Old World.

During the last ice age, which began about 70,000 years ago, much of the earth's moisture accumulated in ice caps and glaciers. Sea levels gradually dropped as much as almost 500 feet, exposing the Bering land bridge, a landmass more than 1,000 miles wide from north to south connecting Asia and North America.

An Ice Age culture called Upper Paleolithic extended from western Europe and northern Africa across Asia. Paleolithic hunters in Siberia moved onto the vast steppe of the land bridge in pursuit of game. Large stone spear points suggest that their intended prey were massive animals such as woolly mammoths and long-horned bison, but they would also have eaten shellfish, birds, and eggs.

Some experts believe people came to North America from Asia as early as 40,000 B.C. —about the same time as other people moved into Australia—but evidence remains inconclusive. Archaeologists do know that by 12,000 B.C. bands of hunters had moved across the North American continent. The first Americans, then, arrived relatively late in world prehistory.

By about 10,000 B.C. melting glaciers had caused the sea level to rise, and the land bridge had disappeared. Migrating bands of hunters had spread as far as the tip of South America. Large Ice Age mammals became extinct. People adapted to a variety of regions and hunted smaller game.

Also around 10,000 B.C. a hunting innovation—a new kind of stone tool—swept North America. Archaeologists named the complex of tools after the town near which it was first discovered—Clovis, New Mexico.

"Clovis points were flaked on both surfaces. They made easily hafted, very sophisticated, and better killing weapons," archaeologist Dennis Stanford of the Smithsonian Institution told me. "This bifacial technology is not found in Asia. I think it was truly North America's first major development and technological breakthrough. You can use a Clovis point as an efficient knife, so you can do two jobs carrying one tool. I think the idea of this new tool kit moved from one group of people to another very rapidly.

"I believe Clovis mammoth hunting meant winter encampment and all the social things necessary to keep a group functioning. If a band of 25 people killed a mammoth in late fall, they'd have up to 10,000 pounds of meat. I believe they would freeze it, using the hide as a cache protector, set up winter camp next to the kill, and live off it all winter."

After the demise of the Clovis culture, people of the Folsom culture pursued bison in the western grasslands of what is now the United States. Excavations at the Stewart's Cattle Guard site in Colorado have revealed remains of a Folsom encampment of around 8800 B.C. "We've reconstructed that several families, perhaps more than five, killed around twenty animals, camped, butchered the meat, and repaired tool kits," said Dennis. "The last thing they did was crack open the bones for marrow and make a heck of a mess. I'd guess they stayed about a week.

"I think nomadic Folsom people moved from kill to kill in bands of 25 to 50 people at most, exploiting about 9,600 square miles within a few years. My studies show they were territorial and used local raw materials, but some materials passed back and forth between areas, and that indicates contact. Folsom base camps—kingpin places people returned to—became the only analogy to settlement at that time, and in all cases they are associated with a stone quarry."

One such quarry, Alibates, lies about 35 miles north of Amarillo on the Staked Plains of the Texas Panhandle. There, amid sagebrush and yucca, bulk outcrops of flint striated in colors ranging from white, yellow, and red to blue. Work areas dot nearby hilltops. Flint chips lie scattered about, and broken or discarded tools have been found several miles away.

Clovis people utilized and traded flint; Folsom and subsequent cultures also sought the razor-sharp material. Artisans seem to have preferred brightly colored flint, but whether they did so for aesthetic reasons or mystical ones remains unknown.

"Certainly Clovis people had ceremonies," Dennis Stanford told me. "We find cremations and burials with red ocher or offerings of stone points. We know they gathered up bison skulls, probably for ceremonies. Such objects at one Colorado site were remarkably similar to those used in later Plains Indian rituals. I'm sure there were even rituals and sacred places on the land bridge, but evidence of that is something we'll never find."

Perhaps on the land bridge bands of hunters believed that a

Field director Pegi Jodry of the Smithsonian Institution uncovers bison bones discarded by nomadic hunters 10,000 years ago in the San Luis Valley in Colorado. Archaeologist Dennis Stanford and field assistant Barbara Mumford work nearby. Tools—such as the spear point fragments and flaked knife at right— often mark locations where hunting bands sharpened stones and butchered kills.

flood once covered the earth. Perhaps even then they told of a time long before when animals talked to one another and to people. Perhaps children learned that stars were all the animals and people who had lived before; that trees, stones, even glaciers harbored spirits. Those ancient hunters must have been namers of mountains and makers of myths—cosmic visions brought down to human scale. Some scholars believe many traditions of today's Native Americans trace back to Asian roots.

"Ancestral spirits, sacred landscape, and communication with the forces of nature are shared American Indian attitudes," art historian Richard F. Townsend of the Art Institute of Chicago told me. "I think they are ultimately deeply rooted in Paleolithic life. Look at the way Australia's Aboriginals think about sacred geography. Every rock, every tree, every cave and gully is a place invested with memories of origin times and the deeds of ancestors, mythological heroes, and adventures of the tribe. They lack great monumental art, but the land is their icon, and they have invested it with layers of cultural meaning. That's useful to bear in mind when thinking about original beliefs in the New World.

"Harnessing ecological resources and expanding the economy are primary forces in the development of societies and their increasing complexities, but parallel with that is the idea of sacred places. With the growth of cities and state organizations, the concepts of landscape and cosmos and religion became more

17

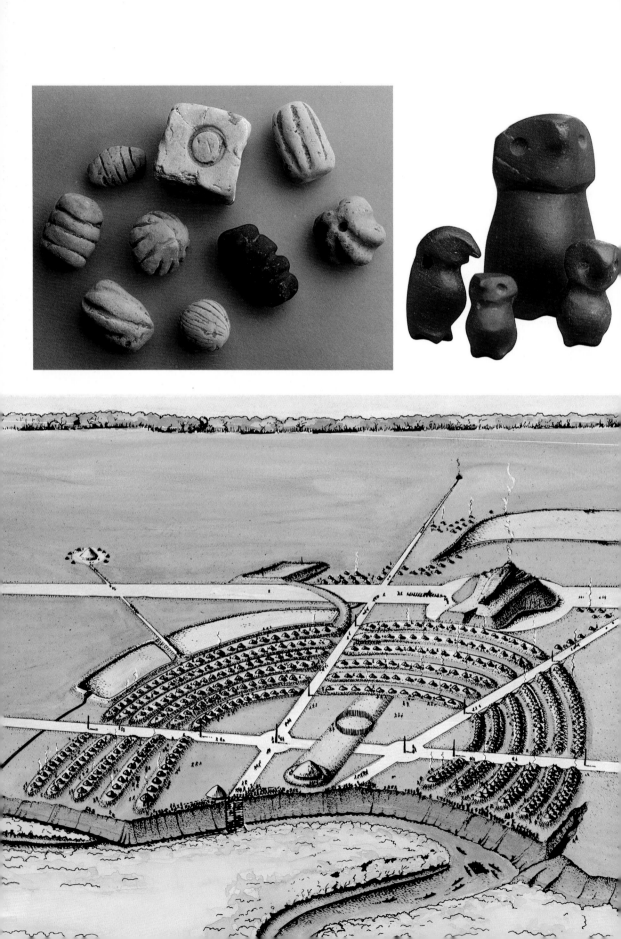

elaborately represented in the visual arts, but fundamentally they seem to be manifestations of something all have shared."

Generally, only settlements with surplus food could afford the time and labor to represent sacred landscapes visually, and they flourished with the rise of agriculture. Mesoamericans were probably the first to grow corn—the seeds of New World civilization. Small cobs found in Mexico's Tehuacan Valley date from about 5000 B.C. Knowledge of maize cultivation may have existed in other tropical areas as well. From there it spread slowly northward. Corn agriculture did not extend throughout the Eastern Woodlands until around A.D. 500 to 800, but there, 2,000 years earlier, a mysterious people began developing a complex culture.

By 1500 to 1000 B.C., the culture archaeologists call Poverty Point permeated parts of present-day Louisiana, Arkansas, and Mississippi, encompassing independent groups that probably spoke different languages. These peoples manufactured and traded artifacts made from exotic rocks and minerals. Small villages in each area were focused on larger centers, but the cultural capital was the Poverty Point site in northern Louisiana, a hub of trade with contacts from the Great Lakes to the Gulf of Mexico.

Several thousand people lived in the town of Poverty Point. There they built five or more earthen mounds, two of which may be massive bird effigies. They enclosed a ceremonial plaza in six concentric ridges that stood as high as eight feet and totaled more than seven miles in length—the largest architectural and engineering project north of Mexico at that time.

"A fistful of folks and simple tribal organization might have managed the work over a long period, although I have difficulty imagining what might have sustained commitment and motivated labor century after century," said archaeologist Jon Gibson of the University of Southwestern Louisiana. Jon believes a hierarchy of powerful leadership had likely developed into the first chiefdom north of Mesoamerica. It was probably the first community "to rise above its contemporaries and start the long journey to becoming a truly advanced society."

Some experts suggest that its rise occurred independently. Although there is no indication of farming, Poverty Point people enjoyed a bounty of wild food, which enabled them to prosper. Others believe the culture sprang from Mesoamerican ideas or even from Mesoamerican immigrants bringing a dynamic way of life and a new religion. While Poverty Point people were constructing earthen mounds and ridges, the Olmecs of Veracruz were building Mesoamerica's first great earthworks.

Whatever Poverty Point was, it grew from inspired effort and reached a new level of development. But sometime after 1000 B.C. the grand experiment began to fail. Perhaps Poverty Point happened before its time. For unknown reasons it could not be sustained, yet with its widespread influence and monumental works, it anticipated urban glories still to come. ∎

Earthworks of Poverty Point border the banks of Bayou Macon in northeastern Louisiana. Built 3,000 years ago, ridges topped by thatched dwellings curve around a central plaza; a ceremonial mound, nearly 700 feet in both length and width, crowns the site. Grooved clay stones—once heated for pit-oven baking—and clay owls one to four inches high exemplify villagers' handiwork. After about 1000 B.C., farming and fishing gradually supplanted hunting and gathering and led to a more settled life for peoples of eastern and southwestern America.

ART BY JON L. GIBSON,
TINTED BY VIVIANE Y. SILVERMAN

19

OZETTE
Arctic Ocean
CANADA
U.S.S.R.
Bering Str.
Alaska
(U. S.)
Bering
Sea
KARLUK
CRAG POINT
Kodiak I.
Pacific Ocean
0
500 km
0
500 mi
MAP ART BY TIBOR G. TOTH
KNIFE RIVER SITES
ON-A-SLANT VILLAGE
UNITED
MESA VERDE
San Luis
Valley
BETATAKIN
AND KEET SEEL
CHACO CANYON
SANTA CLARA PUEBLO
ALIBATES FLINT QUARRIES
GRASSHOPPER PUEBLO
ACOMA
CLOVIS
SNAKETOWN
GILA CLIFF DWELLINGS
CASAS GRANDES
Gulf of California
Pacific Ocean
MEXICO
0
300 km
0
300 mi

CANADA

STATES

●LAWSON

NEWARK
●
●MOUND CITY

●CAHOKIA   SERPENT MOUND

TOQUA AND CHOTA
●

SPIRO

●ETOWAH

●MOUNDVILLE

●
POVERTY POINT

Atlantic Ocean

Gulf of Mexico

The maps locate sites north of central Mexico referred to in this book.

The Eastern

WOODLANDS

Stand in one of the surviving shapes at twilight, when the site lies deserted and silent.

S wift, deep, and powerful, the Scioto River coursed between venerable trees and past a group of ancient manmade mounds ranged along one side. It rushed toward nearby Chillicothe, Ohio, and plunged southward to join the mighty Ohio River. Sycamores, cottonwoods, and maples—arboreal sentinels of its passage—appeared dressed for some forgotten autumn ceremony, in brilliant foliage heralding the decline of the year.

A mantle of summer-green grass still covered the mounds, but skeletal leaves shattered beneath each footfall. Autumn, when nature's cycle of growth and maturity comes to an end, seemed an appropriate time to visit the site, officially called Mound City Group National Monument, but historically known as the City of the Dead.

Today, 23 restored mounds, surrounded by an earthen embankment that encloses 13 acres, form a 2,000-year-old cemetery—a window on the classic Hopewell way of life, which materialized in southern Ohio around the beginning of the Christian era. Ohio Hopewell influence extended along the western flanks of the Appalachians from present-day New York to Georgia and Florida. An Illinois variation called Havana-Hopewellian spread far afield, from Michigan to Missouri and Kansas, and from Wisconsin to Mississippi. As people and ideas dispersed, the Hopewell produced one of prehistoric North America's most magnificent art styles.

At one mound a glass wall permits a view of the interior, and I bent low to peer inside. The cremated remains of four people lay in a large, shallow basin lined with shimmering mica from the Appalachians. This mound had yielded other burials and grave offerings, one a copper headdress in the shape of a bear whose hinged ears had once bobbed in a wearer's rhythmic dance.

Richness of mortuary goods indicated rank in Hopewell society. At some sites, freshwater pearls by the thousand honored leaders of elite families. In one burial, nearly 300 pounds of obsidian denoted the person's rank as well as his power in the trade or use of the volcanic glass; he may in fact have been a master chipper of spear points. Animal-shaped pipes, interred perhaps with master craftsmen, may have served as clan symbols or held supernatural meaning.

Hopewell followed an earlier burial-mound culture called Adena, which thrived from 600 to about 100 B.C. Although influenced by its predecessor, Hopewell reached an inspired florescence. What compelled these people to achieve such astounding ceremonial complexity? They seem to have expended their greatest efforts on burial rituals and offerings and found their highest expression in them, and so for decades Hopewell was called a cult of the dead. But recently scholars have taken another look and have discovered new clues to mysterious lifeways thousands of years old.

Hopewellians did not simply bury their honored dead. First they cleared and smoothed the ground, and then they usually laid down a floor of earth, sand, or puddled clay. Next they built ceremonial wooden charnel houses and placed the dead inside. At a time they deemed appropriate, they dismantled the houses or set fire to them, and then covered the remains with layers of earth. Originally, a layer of smooth river stones capped each mound at Mound City. Archaeologist Robert L. Hall, of the University of Illinois at Chicago, and others suggest that some Hopewell used a covering of muck "as a life symbol, based on its relationship to the life-giving river."

Hopewell societies built thousands of burial mounds, but Hopewell was not a death cult, as was once believed. Although ceremonies honored the dead, perhaps they also renewed creation and celebrated life. It may be that burial meant rebirth, a reaffirmation of the life cycle, the Earth Mother, and fertility.

Hopewell, scholars say, should not be considered one culture and cannot simply be called a religion. Rather, it should be viewed as a compelling concept that included respect for the powers of nature and influenced many aspects of life for Eastern Woodland peoples.

This Hopewellian concept was held by different groups, and its manifestations varied from society to society. There was never an overall Hopewell leader, for each village had its own chiefs and ceremonies. Hopewellians engaged in diplomacy and trade,

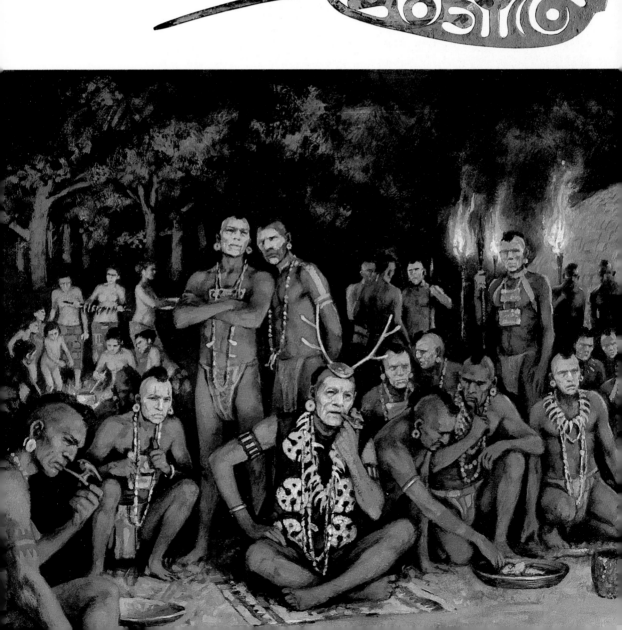

Artifacts from burial mounds express the importance of nature in Hopewell life. Carved from stone, a bird perching on a fish becomes a pipe. Copper hammered into a thin sheet and cut out depicts a fork-tongued serpent. The translucent bird claw at right was fashioned from fragile mica.

Arrayed in a feather cape and a copper headdress adorned with antlers and pearls, a Hopewell shaman raises an offering of food at a burial feast. Near a mortuary house, adult male members of the tribe mourn and honor the dead, a man of high rank. Some smoke animal effigy pipes, while others eat meat prepared by women at the cookfire. Many wear face and body paint. Torchlight reflects from copper breastplates and earspools, and glances off necklaces of shell beads, bear teeth, and animal jaws. Turtle shell rattle and drum—a water-filled pot—keep time for dancers.

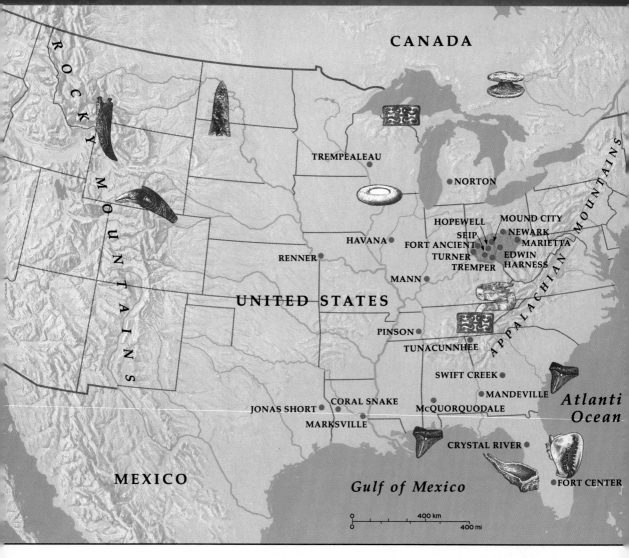

CANADA

ROCKY MOUNTAINS

TREMPEALEAU

NORTON

HOPEWELL   MOUND CITY
SEIP   NEWARK
HAVANA   FORT ANCIENT   MARIETTA
RENNER   TURNER   EDWIN
TREMPER   HARNESS

MANN

UNITED STATES

PINSON

TUNACUNNHEE

APPALACHIAN MOUNTAINS

SWIFT CREEK

MANDEVILLE

*Atlanti
Ocean*

JONAS SHORT   CORAL SNAKE
McQUORQUODALE

MARKSVILLE

CRYSTAL RIVER

FORT CENTER

MEXICO

Gulf of Mexico

0   400 km
0   400 mi

*Spreading their culture as they went, Ohio
Hopewell traders journeyed far from home in
search of exotic raw materials, especially for
ornaments and ritual artifacts. For spear
points the Hopewell imported obsidian from
Yellowstone and chalcedony from the Knife River
region; they also used obsidian for blades. Copper
for ornaments and ceremonial axes came from the
Great Lakes and the southern Appalachians.
Jewelry required silver from Ontario, bear teeth
from the Rockies, shark teeth from Atlantic and
Gulf shores, and shells—also used for vessels—
from the Florida coasts. Artisans fashioned mica
from the southern Appalachians into effigy
objects. Galena from the upper Mississippi
Valley was ground up for face and body paint.*

MAP ART BY TIBOR G. TOTH

● HOPEWELLIAN SITE

OBSIDIAN
BLADE
    CHALCEDONY
    SPEAR POINT

    SHARK
    TOOTH
    PENDANT

    WHELK SHELL
    VESSEL

COPPER PLAQUE

    CASSIS
    SHELL

    SILVERED
    EARSPOOL

    MICA
    SERPENT
    EFFIGY

CARVED
BEAR TOOTH
PENDANT

    STONE CUP
    WITH GALENA
    PAINT

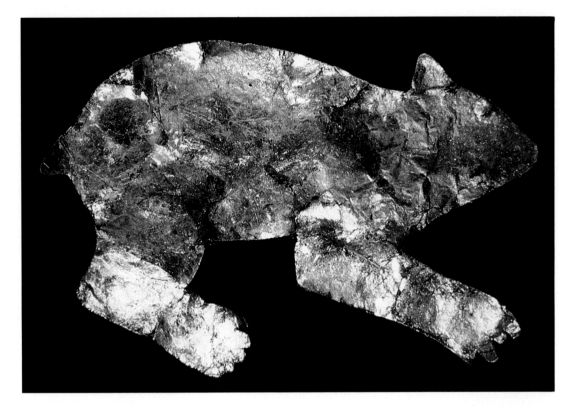

for ceremonial art required exotic goods. Far-ranging traders
would have set out along trails already ancient, or boated along
rivers, those superhighways of prehistoric times. They sought
valued materials, among them copper from the Great Lakes and
the Southeast, obsidian from the Yellowstone region, shells from
the coasts of Florida, and silver from Ontario.

Yet despite their extensive trading activities, Hopewellians
never built great cities. Their largest settlements never had more
than 400 people. Most lived in small villages, hamlets, and home-
steads. They gardened on a small scale, growing squash, domes-
ticated local plants, and in some places tobacco—but agriculture
was not yet a way of life. Hunting, fishing, and gathering remained the basis of their food economy.

"Actually, we know little about their settlements," archaeologist N'omi Greber, of the Cleveland Museum of Natural History, told me. "Much has been destroyed, built over, plowed over.
It's the earthworks they built that we know best."

The earthworks at Newark, Ohio, are among the most impressive examples of Hopewell engineering. The town has oblit-
erated most of them, but 19th-century maps and 20th-century
aerial photographs reveal their former extent. Several groups of
geometric configurations lay in a fertile area where two streams

Skin of a bear, its skull a headdress, cloaks a Hopewell medicine man. The head in the lap of the stone figure may signify preparation for burial, since the Hopewell often dismembered their dead.

6¼ INCHES HIGH

converge. Parallel embankments formed causeways joining a 20-acre square to a gigantic oval, a 20-acre circle to a 50-acre octagon. Some causeways linked the groups, which together covered an area of perhaps four square miles.

Stand in one of the surviving shapes at twilight, when the site lies deserted and silent. Grassy embankments encircle you and shut out the world and time. The place gives you an emotional jolt. You sense the vigor of the Hopewell people and the power of their inspiration. Why, you might wonder, did they build geometric earthworks?

Spectacular ceremonies doubtless took place in them, for burial mounds lie within some shapes. Octagon, circle, and square may have symbolized different clans, just as owl, wolf, bear, and other animals often did among American Indians, or the shapes may have held mystical meanings as yet unknown. Perhaps a specific clan met within a certain shape. Causeways would have allowed movement, maybe for gatherings of clans at auspicious moments. N'omi Greber and other experts are investigating the possibility that earthworks served as a system of astronomical alignments for sighting and marking events such as equinoxes and solstices.

How did the Hopewell execute these masterpieces of earthen architecture? James A. Marshall, a civil engineer in Illinois, has surveyed, mapped, and analyzed more than 200 sites in the eastern United States, and concludes that Hopewellians were "master earth measurers." He theorizes that they first made plans to scale, just as modern architects do. Next they staked out a formal grid, using a 57-meter standard measurement, which demonstrates a knowledge of geometry. "There existed among the Hopewell a 'school of mathematics' whose musings on geometrical concepts differed from the Pythagoreans of ancient Greece only in degree," says Marshall.

Hopewell people probably built most of their earthworks before A.D. 300, and soon their way of life collapsed. No one knows exactly why. Climatic change or interruption of trade may have helped eclipse their glory. Scattered groups continued to build burial and effigy mounds, but centuries elapsed before a movement on such a grand scale swept the Eastern Woodlands again.

By around A.D. 500 to 800, the spread of corn agriculture throughout eastern North America signaled the end of what archaeologists call the Woodland period. Some think corn agriculture came north directly from Mexico; others believe it took an indirect route from Mesoamerica. "Corn was in the Southwest in 1000 B.C.," archaeologist James B. Griffin, a research associate at the Smithsonian Institution, told me. "I believe it spread from there along the Canadian, Red, or Arkansas River into the East—but the precise route is not known."

Populations increased, and they embraced a new way of life, which archaeologists call Mississippian. It began in the lower

Mississippi Valley around A.D. 700 and gradually spread north into what is now Wisconsin, west into South Dakota, east through the Carolinas, and south into Florida. Mississippian cultures, with regional variations, endured in these areas for nearly a thousand years.

From mixtures of clay and crushed shell, Mississippian people made distinctive forms of pottery. They used bows, and arrows tipped with small stone points. They engaged in long-distance trade and intensive agriculture, and became increasingly territorial and warlike. Mississippians embraced a complex ceremonialism keyed to the fertility of the earth and the benevolence of the sun and cosmos. They continued the earlier practice of building burial mounds, but now earthen platform mounds used as substructures for temples, council houses, and dwellings of the elite were ranged around plazas. Perhaps most significantly, organized chiefdoms dominated Mississippian life.

"In areal extent of influence, ceremonialism, public works, technology, population density, and general richness, the Mississippian is exceeded by no other aboriginal American culture north of Mexico," wrote archaeologist Jesse D. Jennings.

Mississippian people constructed the continent's largest prehistoric settlement—and perhaps its only true ancient urban center—outside of Mesoamerica. The ruins, at Cahokia Mounds State Historic Site near Collinsville, Illinois, lie about six miles from the Mississippi River in the widest and most fertile part of the floodplain, the American Bottom. I visited Cahokia on a summer morning of steady drizzle, a time when hard outlines soften, an air of mystery permeates the landscape, and gray tones bind earth to sky.

With archaeologist and site interpreter William Iseminger, I climbed the reconstructed log steps of Monks Mound, the largest earthen structure north of central Mexico. Begun around A.D. 900 and completed 300 years later, it has 4 terraces; rises 100 feet; covers some 16 acres with a base measuring approximately 700 by 1,080 feet; and contains about 22 million cubic feet of earth. Sample cores taken from the mound revealed multiple construction stages. Each had been built by mass labor—hundreds of workers bringing basketload upon basketload of dirt from nearby borrow pits. A building, gigantic by Mississippian standards, once stood on top; it measured about 100 by 48 feet and perhaps towered more than 50 feet. It may have been a temple, a council house, the ruler's house, or a multipurpose structure.

Bill and I sat on the topmost step, surveyed remains of the plaza and mounds below, and in conversation brought ancient Cahokia to life. "The city reached its peak between A.D. 1000 and 1200," Bill explained. "Estimates of its population at that time

Rising sun of the autumn equinox aligns with a wooden post inside a reconstructed sun circle set in ancient post holes at Cahokia. Archaeologists speculate that the formation, 410 feet in diameter and nicknamed Woodhenge, may have helped establish an accurate calendar.

range from 8,000 to more than 42,000. I think it was somewhere in between—about the same as contemporary London. Originally Cahokia covered close to 4,000 acres and had more than a hundred mounds. The log stockade, a defensive wall with bastions, was rebuilt at least three times over a period of about 200 years. It protected this central and probably most sacred part of their community. It also may have been a barrier between social classes. Most likely the upper class lived inside the stockade. During an attack the others probably came in to help defend it. We don't know who their enemy was, who they were afraid of, but they kept building this wall."

I asked Bill if Cahokia had developed beyond a chiefdom. "Some people would agree it was at least an incipient state," he said. "But whatever else Cahokia was, it was the biggest center that ever developed north of Mexico and had to have a bureaucracy to manage and maintain it. How much territory it actually controlled is debatable, but its influence extended over several hundred miles." Bill speculates that, given its size and complexity, Cahokia must have had a system of keeping records of population, military activity, tribute, and food production and distribution; but so far no evidence of this has been found.

Bill pointed westward into the mist. "On a clear day you can see downtown St. Louis, about eight miles away," he told me. "There was a satellite community there, with 26 mounds. There was another group where East St. Louis is now, and several other multiple-mound communities were in this area. There were some single-mound communities and many no-mound communities, too." Virtually all have been destroyed over time.

"One reason Cahokia became as big and important as it did was its central location," said Bill. "The Mississippi, Missouri,

34

and Illinois Rivers join near here, and the Ohio's not far away. The Great Lakes lie to the north. It's also one of the main places in the country where major ecological zones come together—prairies to the east, the Great Plains to the west, the Ozark Plateau to the southwest, and the Mississippi Basin to the south. Cahokians had access to many resource zones. Fish and venison played important roles in their diet, and a major migratory flyway runs north and south."

The hum of modern commerce rose from behind Monks Mound as trailer trucks sped to and from St. Louis along Interstate 55-70. The highway overlies the ancient bed of Cahokia Creek, a stream that once carried canoes from the Mississippi River to Cahokia, transporting essentials such as food and also exotic goods such as copper and marine shells for the elite. As in Hopewell times, influential ideas must have arrived along with coveted cargo. In fact, concepts may have been as valued as commodities. "What stories people told, what ideas they exchanged, would far outweigh the presence of pottery," says James Griffin.

I asked Bill Iseminger if he sees Mesoamerican influence at Cahokia. "The platform mounds, the plazas, and a lot of ceramic forms are very reminiscent, but we have no hard evidence of contact," he said. "We'd love to find a piece of pottery that says 'Made in Mexico'! We don't think people migrated here from Mexico. Rather, ideas filtered in, so we see a kind of watered-down version of Mexico. The ceremonies, the rituals that went with planting, tending, and harvesting corn, had Mesoamerican origins, and, as agriculture spread, people had to keep those traditions going, so influence probably came in that form."

Cahokia's astronomical expertise may have developed in place, evolving from ancestral beliefs. Whatever the source, Cahokians moved to the rhythm of the cosmos. "Treating Cahokia as a whole, there is every reason to believe that its builders put to use a well-developed blend of rudimentary astronomy and geometry in planning their city," writes archaeoastronomer Ray A. Williamson. "Instead of being scattered randomly, the placements of the individual mounds give every appearance of having been planned deliberately. Most mounds cluster about the major east-west axis at the site and are roughly oriented along the cardinal directions. The mounds also seem to be grouped to form smaller units of platform mounds, plazas, and burial mounds within the overall city limits."

Bill and I looked far to our right, outside the area where the stockade would have been, at a circle of tall poles rising in the rain. "We call it Woodhenge," he said. "It's a reconstructed sun circle—a kind of calendar system. It has a diameter of 410 feet, 48 poles, and a central observation point. Sunrise positions at equinox and solstice could be observed and calculated. There may have been other astronomical alignments as well, but these aren't fully understood. They built a sequence of at least four

Bauxite effigy about eight inches high portrays a woman tilling the back of a serpent with a short-handled hoe. Unearthed near Cahokia, the so-called Birger figurine represents a goddess of fertility and perhaps also of death.

circles about A.D. 1000. This is the third. Other circles in the sequence had different diameters and different numbers of poles. This indicates they either changed calculations or improved or increased alignments."

Both science and myth have recently cast light on the Mississippian belief system, a mysterious religion that influenced all aspects of life. Two female figurines unearthed near Cahokia in late 1979 and early 1980 spoke to archaeologists through ancient religious symbols. Carved from brick-red bauxite, the figurines had been ceremonially interred at a site where the dead were prepared for burial. Archaeologists named them the Birger and Keller figurines after local landowners.

The Keller female kneels on ears of corn, suggesting agricultural fertility. The Birger figurine also kneels, but on a serpent creature with a feline head that almost encircles her. Gourd-bearing vines grow from the animal's tail onto her back and around a bundle that hangs from a tumpline. She bends to till the serpent's body with a short-handled hoe. Her curled lips and bared teeth may signify death, or they may imply that she belongs to the supernatural world. Like the Keller figurine, she indicates fertility.

Guy Prentice, a graduate student in archaeology at the University of Florida, notes that among agricultural peoples of eastern North America, "Earth-Mother is the mythological mother of all humans and vegetation. She is the womb from which all life originates and to which all life returns with death. She is a symbol of the cycle of life." The serpent in Mississippian art is often associated with death motifs, and in myth it was the source of plant life. Many traditions speak of sacred bundles of fertility and renewal presented by deities. Prentice adds: "It was believed that through the spirits of dead relatives the Creator would help the living; and prayers were offered to her to maintain her beneficence." The Birger figurine, then, may depict "an earth goddess who is also the goddess of death from whom life springs eternal and through whom the lost souls of the dead are reborn."

Rich spectacle must have accompanied rituals honoring such powerful deities and the cycle of the seasons. Pomp and pageantry must have marked birth, death, and other rites of passage for the privileged elite. At times thousands of people would have massed in the sacred center; the sight and sound of them can only be imagined. But after 1250, Cahokia's population declined, for reasons as yet unknown. Rebellion, war, or disease may have contributed; a climatic change in the 13th century may have brought on famine; deforestation and habitat destruction may have eliminated energy sources and game. Cahokia reverted to a village. By 1450 it lay abandoned.

As Cahokia's glory began to fade, Mississippian cultures in other locations had achieved their greatest florescence. Hundreds, perhaps thousands, of smaller communities dotted the

Southeast and the Mississippi River drainage. Three of the largest were Spiro in Oklahoma, Etowah in Georgia, and Moundville in Alabama. Although they never matched Cahokia in population, they engaged in extensive trade and nurtured a sophisticated art style that reflects complex societies.

From a village of modest size and comparatively little distinction, Moundville rapidly evolved into the greatest of these centers, becoming the largest settlement in the Eastern Woodlands after 1250. One archaeologist has called it the "Big Apple of 14th-century North America."

The site, Mound State Monument, sits atop 60-foot bluffs on a fertile terrace at a curve in the Black Warrior River. I visited Moundville most recently when autumn chilled the air, but trees that edge the riverbanks and ring the 20 mounds still wore the green of the Deep South's long growing season. A steady rain had discouraged other visitors, and I wandered alone in the site's more than 300 acres.

I recalled how Douglas E. Jones, Director of the Alabama State Museum of Natural History, had described his favorite time to visit: "At dawn in spring heavy mist often blankets the earth. The mounds rise above it as if suspended." I, too, found early morning mist. It lay within the gorge and shrouded the river. At times it rose up the bank from behind the largest mound and assumed vaporous, swaying shapes. Features formed, moved, and slid into oblivion; wispy arms seemed to beckon, then disappeared. Somewhere mourning doves cooed and jays screamed.

As many as 3,000 people may have once lived in Moundville. The satellite villages that both supported and depended upon it spread along some 75 miles of the river valley, adding perhaps 10,000 subjects or more to Moundville's jurisdiction.

On many ceremonial occasions, people from these villages would have gathered at Moundville, approaching it along well-worn paths. Smoke from the sacred fires rose from thatched temples high on mounds. In the ceremonial plaza below, costumed dancers performed, and crowds cheered players in ball games and other sports. In summer they celebrated the first harvest with the Green Corn Ceremony. They may have watched priests in rich regalia of feathers, shells, and copper greet the sun at dawn. At times they probably participated in purification rites, with sweat baths and "black drink"—an emetic made from holly and drunk from conch-shell vessels.

At the University of Alabama in Tuscaloosa, I talked with archaeologist Vernon James Knight, Jr. "Apart from villages in the valley," Jim said, "sites showing some Moundville influence included those in much of present-day Alabama, part of Tennessee, and part of Mississippi. Moundville itself was in a trade network involving at least the whole Southeast. Pots from the

Mississippi Valley and shells from the Gulf coast are found there.

"We know so much more about Moundville than we did a few years ago," Jim told me. "At one time, Moundville was thought of as a peaceful agrarian empire. That's not true. And now we can even date its growth." Beginning about 1250, Moundville experienced the building boom of a planned community. "I wouldn't be surprised at all if it happened under one dynasty of chiefs," Jim said.

Platform mounds and a tear-shaped pond dot a terrace above Alabama's Black Warrior River. Here, between A.D. 1250 and 1500, Moundville thrived as a political and ceremonial center. Its artifacts often bear symbols of a religious belief system known as the Southeastern Ceremonial Complex. At top, two knotted rattlesnakes encircle a hand-eye motif on a stone paint palette. Above, vessels exhibit the black burnish typical of Moundville pottery.

PALETTE, DIAMETER 12½ INCHES;
POTTERY, C. 4½ TO 6 INCHES HIGH

Archaeologist Christopher Peebles, of Indiana University, and his colleagues discovered residential sections, public buildings, and work areas where beads, pottery, and woven goods were made. All structures were of wattle-and-daub, with thatched roofs. A sweathouse at the edge of the large plaza probably was used for purification, especially after battle or in preparation for sacred rites, and a palisade, its bastions expertly arranged for advantageous crossfire, protected the site. On a

north-south axis, platform mounds of the eastern and western halves of the site form a symmetrical whole.

Only a hundred or so burials—out of some 2,000 that were analyzed—contained ceremonial objects that denote high rank. Goods from burial mounds included display weapons—axes and maces—made of stone and copper. Artifacts such as stone disks and shell gorgets were decorated with a variety of motifs—humans in ceremonial regalia, winged serpents, crosses, and sun circles. Such icons were identified with the elite, who were themselves icons to their people. Elites of the larger Mississippian communities came closer to being royal families than did any other Eastern Woodland groups.

In recent years Jim Knight and other scholars have gained new insights into the Southeastern Ceremonial Complex, or Southern Cult, as a religious movement that propelled Mississippian centers toward urbanism. Its organization, Jim believes, was threefold: The nobility had a monopoly on knowledge of mythological beings and the supernatural aspects of success in warfare; a second group controlled ritual mound building, probably gaining office through merit, not noble descent; a third group, the priesthood, tended sacred fires, performed mortuary rites, concocted ritual medicines, and nurtured a cult of ancestors. Each controlled a vital part of the belief system.

Among the most important Southern Cult metaphors were platform mounds. They represented earth and its relation to the cosmos. A myth found throughout the Mississippian area explains that "Earth is floating on the waters like a big island, hanging from four raw-hide ropes fastened at the top of the sacred four directions. The ropes are tied to the ceiling of the sky, which

FOLLOWING PAGES: Mists of dawn envelop Moundville. The largest settlement in the East after 1250, it served as the center of a chiefdom with perhaps more than 10,000 subjects.

is made of hard rock crystal." Myths point to an upper world above the dome, a place that epitomized order and stability. An underworld of seven levels epitomized disorder and change. Earth island was suspended between them. A historic Cherokee version says, "When the ropes break, this world will come tumbling down, and all living things will fall with it and die. Then everything will be as if the earth had never existed, for water will cover it. Maybe the white man will bring this about."

At propitious times, Mississippian people gathered for massive public works projects. "Basically these were funerals," said Jim Knight. "Not of people, but of mounds. Burial, purification, rebirth, emergence—all of these are connected, and all are expressed by mounds. As symbols of the world, mounds became polluted and in need of purification, so the people buried and reburied them periodically. This accounts for some construction levels that don't amount to much when excavated—they're just thin layers of earth. Mounds also symbolized sacred mountains. They were thought of as hollow, representing caves that myths say the first people emerged from.

"It isn't easy climbing into the heads of these people. But we

In a game of chunkey, Cherokee men race to hurl poles at a stone disk. The one whose pole lands closest to where the disk stops wins a point. The Union flag signifies alliance with the British; white flags mean peace. Spectators place bets on the game, which takes place in 1757 at Chota on the Little Tennessee River. Today, a dam downstream floods the site (below, upper left).

have learned so much more in the last decade. For instance, a few art motifs are abstract and don't have any obvious factual reference. I think they're specific glyphs for water, for the underworld, among other things. I don't know if you want to call it writing, but certain symbols were like glyphs—standard ways of representing concepts, which is writing in a sense.

"Almost all the symbolism in their art has to do with war: mythological monsters, spotted hawks, eagles, antlered rattlesnakes with wings. These also appear in historic Southeastern tradition as helpful in war. Many of these symbols are found over a wide geographical area. The antlered and plumed snake shows up not just here, but also in Mesoamerica and South America. Many myths and other ideas must be thousands of years old—incredibly old—to account for that wide distribution. Similar concepts found in the Southeast and in Mesoamerica—mounds, caves, sacred mountains, rebirth—are older than cultures in both areas. They have to be. Florescent cultures took hold of those ideas and transformed them into something visual."

Ancient symbols—animals, suns, crosses, eyes within hands, skulls and long bones—all have specific meanings and

Plaiting white oak splints, Dinah George of Cherokee, North Carolina, weaves a basket in the manner of her Cherokee ancestors. Nearly 600 years ago, pre-Cherokee people engraved the rattlesnakes on a shell necklace (right) found at Toqua, Tennessee, and the spider and sun-circle motifs on the gorget that hung from its center.

GORGET, DIAMETER C. 3½ INCHES

reflect certain beliefs that each decade of scholarship helps clarify. The motifs occur in varying concentrations at most Southern Cult sites. And discoveries continue in spite of past destruction.

In the 1930s relic miners, having leased the property, pitted, tunneled, and dynamited the Craig Mound at Spiro, Oklahoma. Inside, they discovered one of the greatest stores of Cult ceremonial objects ever found. They brought them out in wheelbarrows and sold them on the spot. The trove included human effigy pipes, stone axes and maces, copper plaques, masks and human figures carved from wood, and conch-shell cups and gorgets engraved with mythological scenes and other religious motifs. Through the years scholars traced most of the objects to museums and private collections and gleaned enlightening facts. Studies of the shell cups alone give insights into Cult minds. Figures shown in distinct costumes probably depict specific deities. Experts even established a chronology for changes in art style on the cups. They found that some vessels had been 200-year-old heirlooms when buried in the mound.

After 200 years of splendor, the symmetry of the Southern Cult crumbled, and the system failed. By the time European adventurers probed the Southeast in the mid-1500s, Moundville, Spiro, and Etowah were inhabited by small groups of people who had no direct knowledge of the centers' former glory.

Yet pockets of Cult ceremony, power, and pomp endured, and eyewitness accounts of them bring the ancient people to life. In the early 1700s, Antoine Le Page du Pratz, a Dutch settler in the French colony of Louisiana, lived eight years among the

47

Natchez Indians. Their ruler, the Great Sun, claimed divine descent from the sun. He wore a crown of white feathers, and his subjects carried him on a flower-canopied litter, a symbol of chiefly rank found at some Mississippian burial sites. "The Natchez," du Pratz observed, "are brought up in a most perfect submission to their sovereign; the authority which their princes exercise over them is absolutely despotic, and can be compared to nothing but that of the first Ottoman emperors."

"Our nation," the Great Sun told du Pratz, "was formerly very numerous and very powerful; it extended more than twelve days journey from east to west, and more than fifteen from south to north." Now some 4,000 people lived in several villages grouped around a temple mound. Only the Great Sun, as chief priest, and other priests could enter the temple. There the sacred fire burned near the bones of former Great Suns. Lesser members of the Sun family served as officials and governed satellite villages. Suns, Nobles, Men of Rank, and their families formed the upper class. All other people fell into a single lower class contemptuously called Stinkards.

Palisade of saplings interwoven with branches creates a protective maze at the Lawson site, a partially reconstructed Iroquoian village of the 1500s in London, Ontario. Stakes in post holes show where longhouses once stood. Above, mirror-image bears form the handle of a bone comb 3½ inches long. Skillfully wrought human, animal, and plant elements grace many Iroquois artifacts.

The Cherokee lived by their own interpretation of the Mississippian way, building mounds as metaphorical mountains in the shadows of natural peaks, tilling fertile valleys, and living in hamlets and towns. The heartland of the prehistoric Cherokee lay within the Great Smoky Mountains, which loom above the clouds like man-made mounds rising out of the mist. The Cherokee held those heights sacred and recalled their creation through myth. They believed that long ago mud covered the earth and all animals lived above the rainbow. They wished for dry land and sent down Grandfather Buzzard: "When he flapped his wings down, they made a valley where they touched the earth; when he swept them up, they made a mountain."

Anthropologists believe the ancestors of the Cherokee were a local people whose roots reached back thousands of years and who were related linguistically to the Iroquois. During earliest colonial times the Cherokee claimed as much as 40,000 square miles of land, from the Carolinas westward into Kentucky.

In the 18th century the Cherokee were the largest southeastern tribe, a nation of as many as 20,000 people living in 60 or more towns in three regions: the Lower towns of South Carolina and northern Georgia, the Middle and Valley towns of North Carolina, and the Overhill towns of Tennessee west of the Smokies. Each town had a peace chief and a war chief. People gathered in the local council house to smoke, talk, listen, and reach decisions by consensus. But there was strife as well. Competition among increased populations for hunting territories and perhaps also for arable land sparked warfare with other tribes. The

Carved into a living tree for an Ontario museum, a mask portrays a giant—the Great Hunchbacked One—grimacing in pain, his nose broken during a struggle with the Creator. A medicine face like this one, Iroquois believe, takes its power from the tree. With their bold and often distorted features, masks remain the most distinctive Iroquois art form.

Cherokee also engaged in battle for the honor it bestowed, and they traditionally skirmished with all their neighbors.

Theirs became a culture of accommodation. The Cherokee quickly adopted European firearms, metal tools, clothing, jewelry, and even house types—log cabins replaced traditional dwellings. They welcomed opportunities for profitable trade, notably in deerskins. To preserve their nation, they struck alliances and misalliances with the British and Americans. Eventually, all such efforts failed. Most of the Cherokee were forced to migrate to Oklahoma in the 1830s. There, descendants of Mississippian tribes still don costumes and ornaments reminiscent of Mississippian cultures to celebrate the Green Corn Ceremony.

The Iroquois culture, like that of the Cherokee, developed from ancient local roots. Myth traced the Iroquois back to a woman who fell from the sky. The Iroquois had star myths, and they told of journeys to other worlds. Their rituals appeased malevolent spirits and gave thanks to benevolent ones.

Between the spirit forces of earth and sky, the Iroquois created their own world—one of farmers, fishermen, and hunters living in settlements of multiple-family longhouses. They practiced slash-and-burn agriculture, and when soil, wood, and game were depleted, they moved their villages near new fields, often every 20 years or so.

Many later villages were palisaded, for Iroquois often fought their neighbors. "Warfare was so ingrained in Iroquois personality, and self-respect so dependent on achieving personal glory, that individualism outweighed the philosophy of peace," writes ethnologist William N. Fenton. Aggressive and expansionist, the Iroquois conquered some tribes and dispersed others.

Northern Iroquoian territory included parts of present-day Pennsylvania, New York, Ontario, and Quebec. In the 15th or 16th century, five tribes—the Mohawk, Oneida, Onondaga, Cayuga, and Seneca, later joined by the Tuscarora—organized themselves into a league or confederacy, a metaphorical longhouse that stretched nearly 200 miles across New York State. Although never numbering more than 22,000, these Iroquois were the strongest native power north of Mexico. In the 17th and 18th centuries they played pivotal roles in relations among the French, Dutch, and British, and served as middlemen between Europeans and other tribes.

After the 13th century no Eastern Woodland center had equaled Cahokia's large urban population; after the 15th century none had matched the Southern Cult's inspired religious glory. But Cherokee and Iroquois towns, though smaller, excelled in other ways—in political alliances, warfare, and trade—and probably surpassed their predecessors in all of these. No other settlements matched their aggressiveness and domination until Europeans, beginning in the 16th century, expanded their empires into North America and, in the end, controlled all. ■

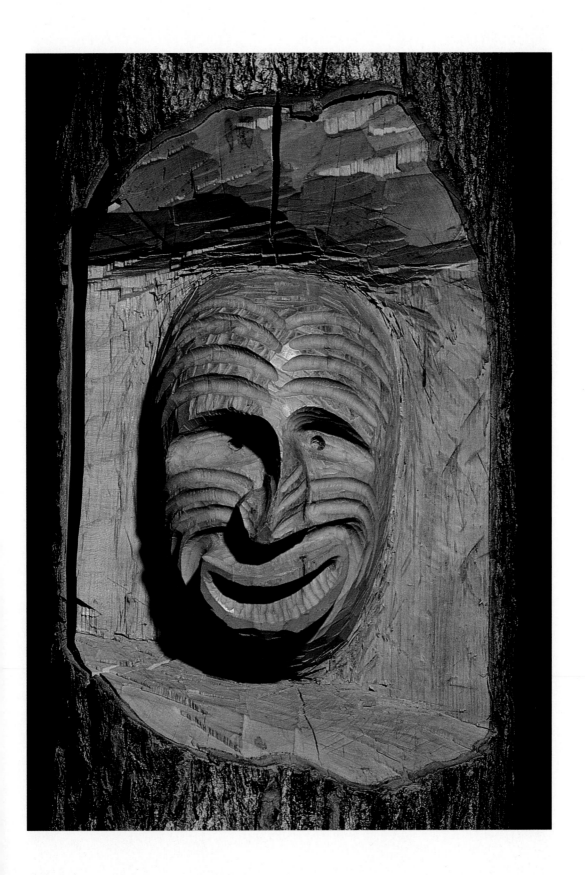

The PLAINS and the

NORTHWEST

. . . supernatural worlds paralleled the physical world and imbued it with an aura of mysticism.

"Walk to the end of the earth," a stranger in Neah Bay advised. "It isn't far." Intrigued with the idea, I set out to hike a trail that pulled me deep into the hushed green gloom of a conifer forest. Velvety mosses covered the woodland floor and crept along low-hanging branches, and ferns filled damp depressions. Moisture permeated the cool air, dripped from leaves, and saturated the spongy ground. As I walked along, the call of an unseen bird occasionally broke the silence.

The trail wound through deep shadows and dappling sunlight, over hills and across bog-spanning footbridges before ending at Cape Flattery—the tip of Washington's Olympic Peninsula and the northwestern extreme of the contiguous United States.

There, at the end of the earth, I braced myself against a cold wind and watched Pacific waves break at the base of the cliff 120 feet below. Just beyond, dark sea stacks slick with spray looked like huge marine mammals turned to stone. A lighthouse on Tatoosh Island, half a mile away, lazily winked a golden eye at an approaching cloud bank.

I knew, as did the stranger in Neah Bay, that this haunting place was the end of the earth only from a local and personal viewpoint. Cape Flattery is but one feature in the rugged terrain of islands, mountains, rivers, and fjord-like inlets that stretches some 1,700 miles along the continent's northwest coast, from northern California to Canada and southern Alaska.

At the end of the 18th century, perhaps as many as 175,000 Indians lived along that coast, attaining one of the highest population densities in aboriginal North America. They generally shared a complex, affluent culture. Archaeologists discovered the most informative sequence of their cultural development just north of Cape Flattery near Canada's Strait of Georgia. There, by 2000 B.C., people living in small inland settlements hunted the

Cannonball Island and shallow reefs shield the mainland ruins of Ozette, a Makah Indian whaling and sealing community on Washington's Olympic Peninsula. A mud slide buried the village five centuries ago, preserving much of its remains and prompting the nickname "America's Pompeii."

FOLLOWING PAGES: Seagoing Makah hunters in dugout canoes return to Ozette with a gray whale in tow—and a heroes' welcome from villagers on shore.

Replicas of a Makah sealing canoe (opposite, at left) and a whaling canoe hold diamond-shaped paddles, harpoons up to 16 feet long, and sealskin floats used to help buoy slain whales. The Makah Cultural and Research Center in Neah Bay, Washington, also houses some 55,000 artifacts from Ozette, including a knob-topped whaler's hat of tightly woven spruce root and cedar bark, bone-and-wood fishhooks, and a mussel-shell harpoon head with cedar-bark sheath (left).

CANOES, 25 AND 31 FEET LONG

forests for deer, elk, and smaller mammals. Skin boats probably gave them limited access to rivers and the sea. By 400 B.C. their hunting and fishing technology had improved, and their wood-working skills were fully developed. By that time, too, their villages of large plank dwellings often covered several acres. Beginning about A.D. 400, Northwest Coast cultures evolved into those described by 18th- and 19th-century European explorers.

Tlingit, Haida, Tsimshian, Kwakiutl, Nootka—scholars usually separate them not by tribe, but by language, and their melodious names evoke the world of ancient seafarers. Through generations these people and their neighbors, living in independent shoreline villages, led lives oriented to the sea. The warm North Pacific Current flowed past with a bounty of fish—cod,

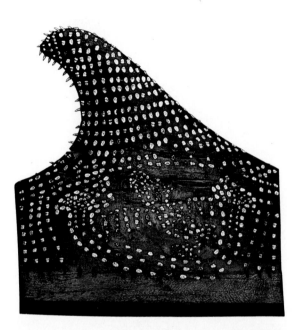

In wolf headdress and button-decorated blanket, John Parker, a Makah, performs his family dance at the Neah Bay center. Behind him, a modern wood carving recalls a prized find from Ozette: a cedar model of a whale's dorsal fin (left), studded with sea otter teeth.

herring, halibut, and salmon—and marine mammals—whales, sea otters, and seals.

In summer the Indians lived in temporary villages near fishing and hunting grounds. From September to May they occupied permanent homes. Winter villages of several hundred people living in large cedar-plank houses dotted riverbanks and seashores. Often villages had as many as four rows, or "streets," of houses. Each house was, in a sense, a hamlet in itself, for several related families lived together under one roof. Partitioned "apartments" with separate cooking fires provided families with minimal privacy. In some villages, towering totem poles with carved symbols proclaimed the lineage of residents.

A web of ranked society bound each village. Individuals knew their place among hereditary chiefs, nobles, commoners, and slaves. Among all North American Indians, no others viewed material wealth as so supremely important. In fact, Northwest Coast Indians have been called the world's most elaborate nonagricultural society.

For them, supernatural worlds paralleled the physical world and imbued it with an aura of mysticism. Geographical features such as mountains and streams held powerful spirits; animals had immortal souls. Salmon were an undersea people who assumed the form of fish and offered themselves to humans as food. Fishermen threw the bones back into rivers, where they were reborn as people to begin the miraculous cycle again.

Most Northwest Coast elites traced their descent from mythical people or animals and received from them the right to certain emblems, songs, and myths. Propitious marriage alliances and even enslavement of rival elites strengthened privilege and power. Rituals and ceremonies brought the physical and supernatural worlds into balance and reinforced rank. One ceremony, the potlatch, honored the host family and obligated visiting nobility to reciprocate with ostentatious feasts and treasured gifts ranging from blankets and wood carvings to canoes and slaves. The distribution, accumulation, and redistribution of gifts played a vital part in elite economy.

The potlatch tradition remains essential to family honor among tribes in Washington State. Neah Bay is the main village of the modern Makah Indians, the southernmost group of the Nootka. There, photographer Rik Cooke attended a potlatch that celebrated the ceremonial naming of two young brothers.

"Everyone who came was given something," Rik told me. "Older people, especially, received valuable gifts. There were more than a dozen handmade quilts, 40 to 50 blankets, household appliances, hundreds of bead necklaces, whole hams and roasts, and dollar bills—they symbolize blankets. I must have received ten bills, each in a formal presentation. The family prepared for the potlatch for two years, and it lasted for hours—with gifts, a feast, costumed dances, and songs that sounded like

"Carve without a past and you carve in a vacuum," says wood-carver Greg Colfax (opposite), a Makah whose exuberant style draws on the traditional arts of northwest tribes. His sun mask reflects the bold colors and curving shapes favored by British Columbia's Bella Coola. Some Colfax works find inspiration in Makah ivory combs discovered at Ozette (right).

chants. It was amazing how welcome they could make an outsider feel—hospitality almost to the point of embarrassment."

In ancient Northwest Coast villages, this same need for material goods gave impetus to one of North America's greatest art styles, expressed mainly in wood carvings, textiles, and basketry. An astonishing archaeological discovery has revealed examples of such traditions.

The Nootka, and thus the Makah, were great whalers. Pursuit of the huge creatures was reserved for men of wealthy families and was a tradition probably at least 2,000 years old. Some 15 miles south of Cape Flattery the ancient Makah beachfront village of Ozette lay closer to the migration route of whales than any other, making it one of the major whaling villages south of Alaska for many centuries. About A.D. 1500, probably after heavy rains, disaster struck Ozette. A steep hillside behind the mile-long village gave way, covering houses with thousands of tons of mud. Most residents escaped, and a new village was built.

In 1970 a winter storm lashed the bank in front of the ancient village, exposing artifacts and the planks of a buried house. Richard D. Daugherty of Washington State University began a program of excavation there that lasted 11 years. Eight to twelve feet below the slump he discovered five houses. He excavated three and found their contents amazingly well preserved. "The mudflow in effect stopped the clock at Ozette, leaving virtually everything preserved in place, somewhat as volcanic ash has preserved a record of everyday life in ancient Pompeii," wrote Dr. Daugherty and his associate, Ruth Kirk.

Each house measured 60 to 70 feet by about 35 feet, and each contained treasures of information. By 1979 some 80,000 recovered objects, from baskets and whale bones to halibut hooks and looms, spoke of everyday life more than 450 years ago. Wood chips marked a workshop area. A sleeping mat still lay spread on a bench. A ranking family had lived in a rear quarter of one house —their ceremonial gear, whaling harpoons, and a distinctive cedar-bark hat worn only by the elite all indicate high status. A large whale fin carved from cedar and inlaid with 700 sea otter teeth may have been important in ceremonies. The design may depict a mythical thunderbird that hunted whales and carried them in its talons to its mysterious mountain home.

"My grandfather and his brother were the last people to live at Ozette—they came here in the 1920s," Helma Swan Ward told me in Neah Bay. "My grandfather was a storyteller. I'm a story-teller, too." We sat on a bench in a replicated plank house at the Makah Cultural and Research Center. In the glow of firelight, Helma told legends of a hero and a myth of two stars that came down to earth as men seeking the maidens who had admired them. She spoke of rituals men performed before setting out on whale hunts, of how they bathed first in salt water and then in fresh water at dawn. She lowered her head and lifted it as if she were an ancient whaler praying and spewing water, mimicking the undulating movements and telltale spouts of his sacred prey.

The warm ocean current that flows past Ozette continues northward beyond the lands of the Northwest Coast Indians and past southern Alaska and Kodiak Island. The waters surrounding Kodiak teem with sea life. Averaging 54 inches of rainfall a year, the island's jagged mountains are blanketed with lush growth as green as Alaskan jade and as soft to the eye as velvet.

"It's so temperate we call the area Alaska's Banana Belt," Richard Jordan of Bryn Mawr College told me.

It was the summer of 1986, and bearded, brawny, Alaska-born Jordan was directing the excavation of a house at Crag Point on the shore of Kodiak's Anton Larsen Bay. The house had been part of a village of modest size occupied from around the beginning of the Christian era to 1100. Crag Point is one of several thousand village sites on Kodiak dating from the same period. Trowel in hand and bundled in sweater and down vest against the Banana Belt's August breezes, I joined the crew for a day and scraped dirt from a trash pit filled with the bony remains of ancient repasts—cod and other fish, duck and other birds, seal and other sea mammals.

"Village cultures in southeastern Alaska were the result of these food sources," said Dick. "I often think how less dependable agriculture is. When corn farmers depended on that one

Rich in salmon, Kodiak Island's Karluk Lagoon (below, at left) has harbored permanent settlements for at least 5,000 years. Pre-European villages may have had as many as 2,000 residents.

Owl mask stares anew at the world after emerging in 1984 from an ancient sod house at Karluk. Opposite: Three men in a bidarka—made of gut stretched over a wood frame—turned up in miniature on Kodiak a century ago. Bits of yarn mimic hull seams and lashings on the 20-inch boat. One hunter wears a tiny version of the seal-head helmet on page 53.

At Crag Point on
Kodiak, Native Alaskan
student-archaeologist
Philip McCormick kneels
in the entrance to a scale
model of a Kachemak sod
house. Four times as
large, ancient dwellings
held sleeping platforms,
hearths, storage pits,
and drainage channels.
Opposite: Lip plugs of
ivory and jet join bone
weapon points, all
found at Crag Point.

crop, how difficult it must have been when the crop failed. These people were farmers in a sense—they harvested the sea. If one economic system failed, if the salmon didn't run one year, they fell back on others. They could have lived on the shellfish alone.

"Anthropologists usually view hunting and fishing societies as small numbers of nomadic people living on the brink of extinction, fighting for survival. Those are stereotyped Eskimos. Kodiak Island gives us a new look at Eskimo culture, and we find that people here lived more like Northwest Coast Indians."

Dick has unearthed the full flowering of Eskimo development on Kodiak. "I'm willing to guess that villagers like these at Crag Point were ancestors of the later Koniag Eskimos," he said.

On the southwestern part of the island, where the Karluk River runs from a mountain lake to Karluk Lagoon and the sea, more than 40 village sites dot the shores for some 20 miles. "From about A.D. 1200 to 1300 those villages were somewhat like this Crag Point one," said Dick. "But by 1400 things changed. We

68

Once the staple of Plains life, bison meant food, clothing, shelter—and more—to the Indian. Their bones became tools, their sinews served for sewing, their dung fueled countless cookfires. Prairie grass (opposite) nurtured the one-ton animals, which numbered perhaps 60 million by the mid-1800s.

have archaeological records stacked like layer cakes—in some places occupation layers are 10 to 12 feet deep. Population increased dramatically. Villages doubled in number. House size tripled. We have magnificent prehistoric 'megavillages'! One village has more than a hundred multiroomed houses. Some houses were almost 22 yards long—'megahouseholds' of 40 to 50 people. About 20 people lived in most structures—2,000 people in one village alone. It was one of the most densely populated regions in Alaska. When you consider the small size of contemporary settlements in the Bering Sea area, Canada, and Greenland, this starts looking like prehistoric downtown.

"Why did this happen? Resources, for one reason. The Karluk is still one of the richest salmon rivers in the world. In those days salmon were probably so plentiful you could kick them out of the water, and if you controlled the salmon, you controlled the main food source. Powerful clans controlled salmon or seals or other resources, and they cooperated with one another. But along with the large houses and villages there were still small villages with very few houses, indicating an elaborate society of inequality and differential wealth and power. Late 18th-century Russian visitors reported that the Koniag had hereditary chiefs, commoners, and slaves. I think that was already true by 1400.

"There was also a change in ideology. An outburst of art expressed a religious world view probably related to mythology and ritual. They even carved religious symbols on tool handles. We found small cone-shaped heads with heavy jaws that may represent a deity or a legendary hero. We discovered that a private back room in one house held spooky figurines perhaps used in secret ceremonies. The floor of a large public room was strewn with miniature masks, and feather-shaped wooden bangles once attached to a large mask. I can imagine a costumed shaman dancing, whirling, and these bangles flying off as he performed. Russians said that during December and January the Koniag feasted, danced, and held ceremonies. This strengthened ties and integrated potentially competitive people into their economic and religious systems. Party time relieved tensions. But we also find technology for warfare—weapons and wood-slat armor. The population grew, and then we find competition and defense."

Hunting societies invariably developed rituals and myths centered on prey. The Koniag treasured powerful hunting talismans and performed ceremonial magic to ensure success in whaling. After Russia acquired Kodiak in the late 18th century, the Koniag began hunting sea otters to supply the Russian fur trade. Whaling declined and eventually became a memory.

From a vantage point in the Black Hills of South Dakota, a landscape sacred to Plains Indians, distant bison look like great shaggy whales coursing through a sea of grass. The animals were the principal prey of Indian hunters until late in the 19th century, when they almost became extinct. Plains Indians, like Eskimos, have been stereotyped as nomadic hunters, yet they, too, developed village cultures.

Beginning about 250 B.C., Woodland traditions spread into the plains as traders funneled exotic stones and metals back to Hopewell centers. Hopewell concepts took hold, and Plains people began making pottery, building burial mounds, participating in long-range trade, and experimenting with corn agriculture. About A.D. 1000, as Cahokia approached its greatest glory and its influence spread, a period called Plains Village began.

"Even though tribes spoke different languages, they generally shared a single culture. All of them farmed bottomlands and hunted upland areas," said Francis Calabrese, head of the National Park Service's Midwest Archaeological Center in Lincoln, Nebraska. "The Hidatsa and the Mandan of North Dakota were not intensive agriculturalists, but they were the northernmost practitioners of small-scale farming in North America, growing corn, beans, squash, and sunflowers. They survived the extreme environment because of a dual practice—growing food and hunting bison. If they'd had to depend on horticulture alone, they probably would never have made it, but they had that alternative food source. It allowed large villages to develop.

"Each village was a unit, which is not much different from medieval Europe. There were no states, no larger entities, and not much cohesion among villages, although they had ties of language and past kinship. These were not chiefdoms—Cahokia and Moundville were very different kinds of things. We have to call these tribes. You had a general village chief, a war chief, a chief of the hunt—individuals leading at different times by consensus. If they didn't like the way someone ran things, they got rid of him and appointed someone else. You had no redistribution of food and wealth. It was an egalitarian society operating very effectively and maintaining a large number of people.

"Along the Knife River we found 23 Mandan and Hidatsa sites. Of these, 13 or 14 were major village complexes. You're looking at 2,000 to 4,000 people in each large village, easily. When they got hold of horses by the mid-1700s—traded up from the Southwest—these villagers adapted them into their lifeway. Horses changed their lives a little, gave them more mobility and sped up their hunts, but they never abandoned horticultural village life. Say one-third of the population in a village were men. By tradition each had two or three horses. That means three to four thousand or more horses. Their economic system with the horse became an interesting food problem in itself. It was hard to maintain the animals in a winter environment." Calabrese laughed, adding, "The horses ate a lot of bark."

In winter, Plains villagers moved to temporary wooded sites along river bottoms that provided easy access to fuel, shelter from winds—and bark. During long hunts they lived in tepees, house types of their nomadic neighbors. Permanent summer villages sat high on river terraces.

I visited On-A-Slant Village, a reconstructed Mandan settlement with several earth lodges on a sloping terrace near the confluence of the Heart and Missouri Rivers. Lewis and Clark passed by there in 1804. The site is now part of Fort Lincoln State Park.

"There were seven villages here, each with 2,000 or more people," archaeologist Chris Dill, of the State Historical Society of North Dakota, told me. "They were four to six miles apart—each within sight of others. If one was attacked and set on fire, people in the next villages would see smoke or some sort of raised signal flag. The Mandan were in league, but they had disagreements. Some groups split off. But the Mandan pulled together against the Hidatsa when necessary. The Mandan and the Hidatsa pulled together against the Arikara and the Sioux. Eventually all but the Sioux pulled together against everybody else.

"We're talking about very big settlements. After all, the area where the Knife River villages were had a larger population then than it does now. Each village was a political unit, but if a group from outside the area came in, villages sometimes joined together. Then the next month they might fight with their neighbors about something else.

Bank of a North Dakota stream bears the impressions of circular Hidatsa earth lodges. Unlike Plains Indians elsewhere, the Hidatsa, Mandan, and other Missouri River tribes lived in permanent trading villages, and subsisted through farming and fishing as well as bison hunting.

FOLLOWING PAGES: A 17th-century Mandan community thrives atop a natural terrace of the Missouri River, its men relaxing while women erect a new earth lodge. Cottonwood poles and willow branches form the house skeleton, topped with thatch and a layer of packed earth or sod. In the distance, cultivated fields furrow rich bottomland—as traders and fishermen ply the water in small, round bullboats of bison hide.

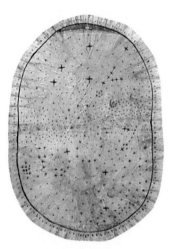

Pawnee star chart of painted buckskin depicts heavenly bodies vital to the tribe's mythology of creation. Scholars believe the chart was part of a sacred bundle—a sort of portable altar containing various relics and used in planting and hunting ceremonies. But its exact purpose and even its age remain obscure, its lore lost to time.

22 INCHES LONG, FIELD MUSEUM OF NATURAL HISTORY, RON TESTA

"These people were great traders. Their villages were hubs of trade networks way back in the prehistoric period. When fur traders came in the late 18th century, they added goods and changed the flavor, but they walked into a system that had been pulling in exotic goods prehistorically. Villagers had traded food they grew to nomadic tribes and probably exported flint. They imported copper and Gulf of Mexico shells. We find Southern Cult decorated shells here that you could lose if they were mixed in with a collection of Cult material from the South."

When artist George Catlin visited a Mandan village in 1832, he noted: "I have this morning, perched myself upon the top of one of the earthcovered lodges . . . and having the whole village beneath and about me, with its sachems—its warriors—its dogs—and its horses in motion—its medicines (or mysteries) and scalp-poles waving over my head . . . its green fields and prairies, and river in full view, with the din and bustle of the thrilling panorama that is about me. . . . There are several hundred houses or dwellings about me, and they are purely unique. . . ."

Rounded and golden, the earth lodges of On-A-Slant Village repeated the shapes of surrounding hills. "About A.D. 1000, there were people in North Dakota living in rectangular earth lodges arranged in rows," said Chris. "We don't know why, but about 1600 they went to these circular domed houses randomly organized. That meant some change of view, a different perception of the world. Also at this time village populations jumped."

Chris and I stepped from brilliant sunlight into a shadowy one-room lodge. "With a two- or three-foot covering of beams, grass, and earth, lodges were cool in summer and warm in winter," he explained. "In an average year temperatures range from 45 degrees below zero to 102 above. Imagine a blizzard raging outside. Eight to ten people lived in each house. There was dirt falling from the ceiling, smoke rising from the fire—the wind pattern inside was tornadic even with a windscreen. Everyone sitting around the fire had a station, and the most important person sat in back where it was least smoky. Then there were children running about, and maybe open storage pits for food or garbage. They roped off an area in the house for their best horses and also brought the dogs inside."

Outside, in the plaza, a low palisaded fence encircled a cedar post commemorating the mythical wooden tower Mandan ancestors built to save themselves from a deluge. "They always had that," said Chris. "It's called the Ark of the First Man. It comes from myths about the flood and the origin of the earth and the first people. I don't know of any Native American group that doesn't have some version of the flood myth."

Plains village religion also reflected dependence on the two principal food sources, bison and corn. For protection against enemies, warriors wore amulets of corn into battle. Corn and bison skulls often adorned household altars.

The Pawnee, living in present-day Nebraska, showed more Mississippian influence than did their northern neighbors. Chiefs and priests usually inherited titles in their ranked society. The Pawnee were also geographically closer to the Southwest and Mesoamerica and doubtless drew social and religious concepts from those areas.

Even nomadic Plains tribes in southern Canada and Montana built medicine wheels—segmented circles outlined with stones that were probably used as astronomical observatories. But like cultures in the Southwest and Mesoamerica, the Pawnee also embraced a ceremonial system that encompassed the cosmos. They are remembered as skilled astronomers. The Pawnee earth lodge "served as an astronomical observatory," wrote art historian Gene Weltfish, "and as the priests sat inside at the west, they could observe the stars in certain positions through the smokehole and through the long east-oriented entranceway. They also kept careful watch of the horizon right after sunset and just before dawn to note the order and position of the stars."

Half-Mandan, half-Hidatsa Mary Barthelemy brightens an earth lodge with her beaded dress of buckskin as she ties a rawhide bag for storing pemmican. Dried corn and wild turnips hang above a corn grinder, and farm tools and buffalo robes occupy other spaces in this reconstruction at Fort Lincoln State Park, North Dakota.

77

Annual July powwow at Mandaree, North Dakota, opens each day with a Grand Entry parade (below). Dancers later vie for prizes in such categories as the Grass Dance (opposite), often performed to recall past hunts or other memorable deeds. The gathering draws tribes from all over the northern plains. Says one participant, "It is a time . . . to teach children to share in our culture."

In the beginning, the Pawnee believed, Heaven, the Creator, sat in the undifferentiated cosmos. He placed a star in each of the four world directions and assigned them power to create people and give them sacred bundles.

A tribal bundle contained objects such as the skull of a leader, a rock crystal, or feathers of certain birds. Forces within the bundle drew upon a universal ocean of power, and this power determined village success.

"There are certain striking analogies between the tribal bundle of the Plains and the ancient ceremonial centers of the Mississippi Valley," wrote archaeologist Preston Holder. "One might say figuratively that the bundle was a sort of portable ceremonial center on a much reduced scale."

Though not centers on a grand scale, villages of the Plains and the Northwest reached high levels of complexity and sophistication—without intensive agriculture, which in other areas permitted the rise of cities. These northern settlements were centers of the earth for their people. I had heard echoes of that world view in Neah Bay. When I told a young woman I had walked to Cape Flattery, the end of the earth, she looked surprised, then laughed and said, "Funny you should put it that way. I've always thought of it as the beginning." ∎

The SOUTHWEST

"No man can think of us without thinking of this place. We are always joined together."

At first, a visitor accustomed to a cozy world enclosed by trees can be intimidated by the vast southwestern landscape. It is beautiful, but it is not comforting. The sky is so much larger than the earth, a transparent dome of shimmering light resting on the edges of the world. The land becomes a blend of reality and illusion, of nature and the supernatural, just as it did for the ancients. Massive boulders and etched canyons, jagged peaks and stark mesas, appear to be the very bones of the earth. Pinnacles sacred to ancient peoples assume fantastic shapes. Mountains in snowy caps wrap themselves in conifers. Desert mirages of distant oases shimmer with a false promise of moisture. Dust devils dance to a moaning wind, and parched riverbeds flow white with blowing sand.

Anthropologist Alfonso Ortiz, of the University of New Mexico and himself a Pueblo Indian, writes of this land, the native peoples who have lived there, and their bonding with the environment: "Here is the oldest continuous record of human habitation on the continent outside of Mesoamerica, a habitation that has fashioned this region into a humanized landscape suffused with ancient meanings, myths, and mysteries."

A modern man of Taos Pueblo probably echoed attitudes reaching back to the beginnings of human habitation in the Southwest when he said, "The story of my people and the story of this place are one single story. No man can think of us without thinking of this place. We are always joined together."

Prevailing dryness helps define the Southwest and its three major environments: desert, mountain, and plateau. People have embraced and utilized these environments for at least 12,000 years. Arid though the region may be, life-giving rivers flow there, and until 6,000 years ago the climate was less harsh, and the land less barren.

Three areas of the ancient Southwest were home to three major farming societies. People whom scholars now call the Hohokam centered in the northern Sonoran Desert valleys of present-day Arizona, especially along the Gila and Salt Rivers. The Mogollon, named after their heartland, the Mogollon Mountains, lived in southeastern Arizona, southern New Mexico, and the modern Mexican state of Chihuahua. The Anasazi built agrarian villages on the high Colorado Plateau of the Four Corners area, where Arizona, New Mexico, Utah, and Colorado meet, and also lived along the Rio Grande and upper Pecos Valleys of New Mexico.

At times, southwestern peoples interacted with peoples of Mesoamerica, where New World agriculture began. By 1000 B.C. a small-cobbed variety of corn had arrived from Mesoamerica, and hunters and gatherers planted supplementary patches of maize along with other new arrivals—squashes and gourds. Later they added beans to their gardens, as well as improved varieties of maize. The stage for the drama of settled life was set.

Hohokam village life became well established around the time of Christ. Some scholars believe the culture developed from local societies that adopted Mesoamerican ideas. Others think people from Mesoamerica migrated northward, bringing an established agrarian culture with them. Still others believe both may have happened, giving rise to the Hohokam way of life. Southwestern archaeologist Emil W. Haury writes that "there is reasonable agreement that the Hohokam were a northern frontier Mesoamerican society."

The northern Sonoran Desert in Arizona seems an unlikely cradle of culture. Annual rainfall there averages five to ten inches, and daytime temperatures often exceed 100°F. It is an area dominated by sun, sand, cactus, saltbush, and mesquite. In aboriginal times more vegetation covered valleys and more runoff filled rivers, but even then the desert was not ideal farmland. Hohokam living in river areas made the land fertile and productive through a sophisticated technology possibly introduced from Mesoamerica. By the time of their cultural peak between A.D. 800 and 1100, the Hohokam had built hundreds of miles of irrigation canals that led from rivers to villages and fields. These canals represent the most complex and extensive water-control system north of Mexico in prehistoric times.

The Hohokam became so skilled in engineering and environmental control that at first glance they appear to have been

arrogant in their placement of villages. If a preferred site did not edge a watercourse, they built one to it, digging canals as long as ten miles from the nearest river. Main canals led directly from rivers that sometimes ran dry seasonally. These canals were six to ten feet wide, and smaller irrigation channels branched from them. Headgates constructed at canal forks allowed farmers to divert or admit water as needed. The canal projects not only supported increasing populations, but also enabled the Hohokam to grow two crops annually, one planted in early spring using run-off from rivers, the other planted during late summer rains. Hunting and gathering remained important as supplements, and the Hohokam flourished.

"The Hohokam were not one of the world's great societies," Dr. Haury notes, "but they revealed a strain of greatness characterized by a cultural form or style that insured unusual stability. By placing primacy on the earth and by being protective of their environment, they forged a social and economic system that enjoyed 1,500 years of ascendancy."

In the 1930s and again in the 1960s, Dr. Haury excavated the Hohokam settlement of Snaketown near present-day Phoenix, Arizona. He believes a subtle and detailed understanding of environment determined the choice of place. The site lay beside thousands of acres of arable land, about half a mile from the confluence of the Gila River and a creek, in a spot where shallow dug wells supplied potable water.

Larger than most Hohokam settlements, Snaketown covered about 250 acres. Its pit houses of wattle-and-daub construction varied in size and shape over time, and their arrangement followed no apparent plan. The Hohokam concentrated their building efforts on the canal systems. Snaketown's population fluctuated from around a hundred people at the time of the settlement's founding about 300 B.C. to as many as 2,000 around A.D. 1100, when the population probably peaked.

A large informal plaza at Snaketown, in use perhaps as early as A.D. 500 to 700, may have served as an activity area or marketplace for settlements for many miles around. Larger villages such as Snaketown may have controlled smaller communities nearby and determined the construction and maintenance of the canals they shared.

"There was undoubtedly some kind of head chief," says Dr. Haury, "but that need not carry with it all the social and political dimensions of a chiefdom. My guess is the Hohokam were loosely organized and didn't have the societal structure of the more sophisticated groups we see in Mesoamerica."

Hohokam religion and the introduction of platform mounds and ball courts along with assembly plazas may reflect an influx of new concepts from Mesoamerica. The largest ball court at Snaketown covers an area the size of a football field, but those ancient games went beyond sport. In Mesoamerica, ritual ball games perhaps traced the movements of the cosmos and helped ensure the continuation of vital and benevolent cycles. Hohokam mounds may have served as ceremonial dance platforms or supported single structures, possibly residences for leaders. They often reveal layers of construction, just as the mounds of the Eastern Woodlands and the pyramids of Mesoamerica do.

Ceremonial and luxury artifacts came directly from Mesoamerica—among them, rubber balls, copper bells, and mosaic pyrite mirrors. From cotton, introduced in early times, Hohokam weavers produced tapestry, twill, gauze, and openwork resembling lace. The Hohokam also fashioned stone paint palettes and bowls, and clay figurines. Snaketown has yielded more human figurines than any other site in the Southwest—about 1,500, most of them fragments. Some may be portraits of actual people, wearing face paint, feather headdresses, turbans, and jewelry. About A.D. 1000, Hohokam artisans developed a technique for etching designs on marine shells with acid most likely made from the fermented juice of saguaro cactus fruit.

Snaketown ceased to exist as a dominant village between A.D. 1100 and 1200. In surviving settlements, changes occurred in architecture and crafts. These may have been introduced by pueblo-building newcomers, who joined the Hohokam in small, scattered villages. Most people abandoned the Hohokam heartland after 1400, possibly because of the failure of overburdened irrigation systems.

A more varied environment shaped the lives of Mogollon mountain people. Their homeland encompassed an area as large as or larger than those of the Hohokam and Anasazi combined,

Etched shells (top) display a decorative style unique to the Hohokam. Artists applied pitch in patterns or animal motifs and immersed the shells in an acid solution— probably made from fermented cactus juice. As the acid etched the uncoated surface, the designs appeared in relief. A carved stone palette (bottom) held pigments, possibly for body painting.

SHELLS, C. 4 INCHES WIDE;
PALETTE, 9 BY 5½ INCHES

and provided more abundant plant and animal life than the desert did. There, at higher elevations with slightly more rainfall, the Mogollon began farming. Probably there, too, they became the first Southwesterners to practice the art of pottery making, spreading the knowledge to their neighbors.

By 200 B.C., Mogollon people busied themselves with a new and settled way of life. They gathered in tiny hamlets or randomly arranged villages that averaged about 20 dwellings each. They placed their settlements near their fields on safe, high ground—ridges, bluffs, or mesas. Rudely constructed walls helped make them more defensible. The Mogollon also built semisubterranean pit houses and special chambers—perhaps the earliest southwestern kivas, used for ceremonies that kept the people in harmony with nature and their gods.

Neighboring groups probably continued foraging as a way of life, raiding Mogollon settlements and disputing land rights with the agrarian upstarts. Later, as their numbers increased, the Mogollon settled on lower ground near valley streams, where farming was easier. In the valleys they honed their agricultural skills, though they still depended in part on wild food sources. They terraced hillsides, and halted erosion and diverted runoff with lines of stones.

Some scholars view the Mogollon as less dynamic than their Anasazi neighbors to the north. At the same time, they suspect the Mogollon led a complex ritual life. After beginning settled life as innovators, the Mogollon gradually became more imitative. Some of their ways survived, but increasingly, from about A.D. 1100, they blended with energetic Anasazi traits to produce a culture called Western Pueblo.

Western Pueblo populations increased dramatically, and agriculture expanded to support them, aided by newly introduced ditch irrigation. Multiroomed pueblos built of unworked stones set in mud mortar became common. One settlement, Grasshopper Pueblo in Arizona, included some 500 rooms arranged around plazas.

The Western Pueblo architectural style eventually spread as far south as Casas Grandes, a settlement in the Mexican state of Chihuahua. The town originally consisted of about 20 independent single-story house clusters, but around 1205 it was rebuilt into multistoried apartments housing perhaps 2,240 people. Casas Grandes may have begun as an outpost for Mesoamerican traders. It became a major trading, manufacturing, and avicultural center with a system of roads and signaling sites, funneling such valuables as turquoise to Mesoamerica and macaws to the Southwest. With a domain of some 33,600 square miles, it thrived until about 1340.

In the Mogollon area, pottery, too, expressed the dynamic cultural mix. The most distinctive variety developed in the Mimbres Valley of New Mexico. Using Anasazi methods of

Art as a cultural mirror may reflect the fashions of the day in a 10½-inch-high human effigy vessel from Casas Grandes in northwest Mexico. Indian artisans made such polychrome pottery more than 500 years ago, with realistic renderings of hairstyles, clothing, and facial paint.

87

Cliff dwellings sheltered in caves blend with the canyon wall on the edge of New Mexico's rugged Gila Wilderness. Mogollon people, influenced by the Anasazi to the north, built the pueblos between 1280 and 1350.

Classic Mimbres bowl from a burial has a small "kill hole" broken out of the bottom—perhaps to release the vessel's spirit. From A.D. 1000 to 1150 the Mogollon of New Mexico's Mimbres Valley produced such black-on-white pottery with geometric designs and paintings of humans, animals, mythical creatures, and plants. Ceremonial objects (far left) found near the Mimbres area bear similarities to those used in modern Pueblo religion. The two figures may represent spirit beings. Carved rabbit sticks, a mountain lion effigy, and serpents made from roots possibly served in rituals. Twill matting protected the artifacts.

Andreita Harvier takes part in the Corn Dance on Feast Day, celebrated each August at Santa Clara Pueblo in New Mexico. Her wooden tablita headdress depicts a masked human figure holding ears of corn—for centuries the staple crop of Pueblo Indians. Painted artifacts (left) may have been parts of paraphernalia used in Anasazi rituals.

pottery decoration, the Mimbres Mogollon created a style of their own, expressing both mundane and mystical life on superbly executed bowls. These were often used as mortuary offerings to cover the heads of the dead. Most were produced between 1000 and 1150. Of some 7,000 documented examples, about 80 percent bear geometric designs. Stylized humans, animals, mythical figures, and plants on the rest mirror an exuberant physical world and a vigorous supernatural one, leading a present-day artist to call them depictions of a cosmic circus.

J. J. Brody, professor of art and art history at the University of New Mexico, notes that the "fundamental image of Mimbres painting is of a tense universe kept harmonious by the careful and rigid balancing of all conceivable oppositions, particularly those that refer to life and to death."

Ancient peoples of the Southwest probably shared many such concepts, and modern Pueblo Indians hold religious beliefs that echo those of their ancestors, the Anasazi of the high plateau. "The Pueblos see themselves as being inextricably woven into the natural scheme of the entire universe," writes western historian John Upton Terrell. "They are not simply pieces of bone and flesh, not simply possessors of certain faculties. They are those things, but they are also of the sands, the winds, the stars, the plants and grasses, the thunder, lightning, rain, the sun and the moon, and the seasons—everything that is born and lives and dies in the eternal cycle of life."

Like other peoples of the Southwest, the Anasazi developed from a nomadic culture. They began cultivating corn around 100 B.C. They grew dependent on farming gradually, but once planting sticks became as important as hunting implements, they embraced a settled life in villages of from 2 to 50 pit houses, which after a time gave way to multistoried pueblos. After about A.D. 500 their culture evolved rapidly, surpassing others in the Southwest beginning about A.D. 900. It came into full bloom in the high, harsh San Juan Basin in northwestern New Mexico, a land of isolated mesas, dusty washes, and eroding winds.

There, in the 11th and 12th centuries, a distinctive lifeway scholars call the Chaco Phenomenon flourished, influencing hundreds of villages and dozens of large towns scattered across the desert basin over an area of some 25,000 square miles. The hub of this network lay within Chaco Canyon, a gorge about 22 miles long and up to several miles wide. In places, cliffs of sandstone and shale rise more than 150 feet. It seems an incongruous setting for the highest cultural development and the most concentrated move toward urbanism in the ancient Southwest.

The visitor comes upon the ancient multistoried towns before perceiving them, for Chacoans used the orange-, coral-, and copper-colored sandstone of the canyon cliffs to build them, and they merge with their setting. They are nature reformed into elegant structures on a grand scale. The largest, Pueblo Bonito, had more than 650 rooms. An architect estimates that walls in its core-and-veneer masonry contained more than a million dressed stones set in patterns—yet Chacoans covered many of them with adobe or matting. Chaco towns averaged 216 rooms apiece, and these measured about twice the size of other Anasazi rooms. Towns included small kivas for every 30 rooms or so, and usually at least one great kiva with a diameter of more than 50 feet. Virtually all had plazas and high walls. They were spectacular, imposing, closed in upon themselves. Today, a haunting emptiness pervades them.

While they erected towns, Chacoans also dotted the landscape with many small single-story villages of irregular masonry, adding rooms haphazardly and constructing small kivas. A single great kiva sometimes served several modest villages.

Several thousand people may have resided in "downtown" Chaco, although many may have done so only seasonally. This area of concentrated settlement lay within today's 12-mile-long Chaco Culture National Historical Park. I drove along the paved loop that winds through it with park archaeologist Dabney Ford.

"All along the cliff face everything you see that's not a boulder and looks like talus is the remains of construction," she explained. "It's phenomenal. I'd estimate there are 400 to 500 man-made structures in the park, built over a 200-year period. Two are prehistoric masonry ramps—bases of roads coming off the cliff. People probably used a combination of wooden and rope ladders and scaffolding to get up the sheer part of the cliff, and the road continued from there. We don't know yet how many ramps and stairways there were, but just within the park area alone, probably 30 or 40."

Research has revealed a system of more than 400 miles of remarkably straight roads. Most lead to outlying towns and their related villages in the San Juan Basin, but some stretch to the highlands beyond. The main ones average 30 feet in width, and there are several cases of 2 roads running parallel to each other.

"We once thought the roads were purely functional economic structures," said Dabney. "We studied how many calories it took to walk on the desert as opposed to walking on roads. There wasn't much difference! Now we think the roads are just incredibly fancy—straight for no purpose. They lead to the edge of a cliff and a stairway when just ten feet in another direction there is a natural way to get down the cliff. Maybe long, wide roads were built to impress people coming to Chaco. The planning and labor that went into these roads and towns is impressive. We're impressed today. There's no reason why someone a thousand years ago wouldn't have been."

As we approached Pueblo Bonito, Dabney said, "We're looking more and more at these 'apartment houses.' We envisioned them full of people. Now archaeology tells us many of the big rooms may have been used for storage. There are some standard living units, but many had a special function not purely domestic. There wasn't the ratio of people to rooms that you find in a modern pueblo, but even so, this canyon was totally occupied. One Chaco archaeologist, Stephen Lekson, has said that by about A.D. 1075 you couldn't walk anywhere and not be in a field, on a road, or beside an irrigation ditch."

Chaco Wash winds through the canyon, but holds water only periodically. Anasazi farmers thus depended primarily on rainfall and efficient techniques for controlling its runoff. After storms, runoff would cascade down the cliffs into natural or man-made catchment areas. During an hour-long summer rain in 1967, an estimated 540,000 gallons of water flowed from one small side canyon. Some experts see such abundance as the reason for Chaco's amazing development.

Chaco's impressive towns may have been founded by families that had access to abundant water, productive fields, and therefore a food surplus. "In time newly forming groups would find themselves farther and farther removed from direct social linkage with the founder group," writes archaeologist Paul Grebinger of the Rochester Institute of Technology. "During the late ninth and early tenth centuries, as population increased, there was a transformation in social organization." Community

FOLLOWING PAGES: As the sun rises behind a sandstone pillar in Chaco Canyon, an Anasazi sun priest greets it with a prayer offering of cornmeal and crushed shell and turquoise. From this sun-watching station, the priest can forecast the winter solstice 16 days later, according to some archaeoastronomers. Through daily sunrise observations, priests in each pueblo kept accurate calendars for plantings and ceremonies. Historic Pueblo practices provided the basis for this painting.

Series of doorways at Pueblo Bonito (opposite) shows the architectural skill of the Chacoan Anasazi. To build a wall, they used earth-and-stone rubble for the core and faced it with sandstone tablets— a technique known as core-and-veneer masonry. Another legacy of the Anasazi, lavishly decorated pots (above) rest on a wall as twilight illumines Pueblo Bonito.

leaders rose from those founding families, capitalizing on their advantages, Dr. Grebinger suggests. Organization, production, redistribution, and related religious ceremonies controlled by succeeding generations produced a ranked society with differences in status. Pueblo Bonito burials attest to high rank. Grave offerings of one individual included about 14,000 turquoise, shell, and stone beads, some 700 turquoise pendants, 5 jet inlays, a shell trumpet, and a basket adorned with turquoise inlay.

Other archaeologists suggest that the Chaco system developed from contacts with diplomat-traders from central Mexico. Certainly trade played an important role—imported copper bells, macaw skeletons, and Mesoamerican architectural details are not unusual at Chaco sites. Perhaps towns supplied turquoise sought by Mexican traders—yet the closest mines lie more than a hundred miles away. Or perhaps turquoise served as a medium of exchange among the Anasazi themselves. All of these theories may help explain the mystery of Chaco's development.

Despite their proximity, towns evidently had no overall leader. Still, they were linked by networks of roads and signaling stations, and there must have been cooperation on construction projects, a unifying religion, wide redistribution of food, and a great deal of diplomatic activity.

Archaeologist Linda Cordell of the California Academy of Sciences describes Chaco at its peak: "As the Anasazi tended their crops, traders went from village to village, offering news and gossip as well as their wares. Occasionally, perhaps, traders

Prized for their plumage and for ceremonial use, scarlet macaws keep aviculturists busy in the frontier trading town of Casas Grandes. Near rows of nesting boxes, a merchant presents a bird he wants bred. A keeper roasts agave hearts—food for the parrots—in a pit oven. Bird motifs on Kayenta Anasazi ware (opposite) attest the importance of macaws in commerce and ritual.

BOWL, DIAMETER 8½ INCHES;
MACAW EFFIGY VESSEL, 4 INCHES
HIGH; LADLE, 7 INCHES LONG

from the far south were drawn to the bustling towns, offering scarlet-winged macaws for turquoise tessera or beads. At times, processions of men in finely woven kilts and heavy necklaces of shell may have entered the plazas to the measured rhythms of flutes and drums to offer dances for rain and for the good of all the people." Dr. Cordell imagines men and boys weaving and fashioning jewelry and tools in kivas: "While they worked, they would recite and discuss the traditional stories and legends that contained the truths of the Anasazi way of life—the ways of the gods and the ancestors, the habits of mammals and birds, the etiquette of social life, and the organization of the universe."

My routine during a visit to Chaco soon followed the rhythm of the universe. Up before dawn, I watched the first sunbeams play across Fajada Butte, which rises from the canyon floor. The butte caught the last rays at sunset as well, as if it were a gigantic pivot for the orbit of the sun. Rabbits frolicked around a boulder as daylight faded, and a young coyote, its coat the same mottled browns and grays as desert shrubs and grasses, traced the same path and sent the same sparkling glances my way each day as afternoon waned. Venus, as the evening star, rose more brilliant than it had in years to join a full moon.

Down the canyon to the northwest lay the Chaco town of Penasco Blanco. "It's the best place in the area for sunset and Venus watching," archaeoastronomer Michael Zeilik of the University of New Mexico told me.

Ancient symbols painted on rock near Penasco Blanco intrigue Mike and his colleagues. A hand marks the site as sacred, and concentric circles may represent the sun. A starlike shape next to a waning crescent moon may signify a famous celestial phenomenon—the Crab Nebula supernova of 1054, also recorded by people in China, Japan, and the Middle East.

"That supernova was brighter than Venus," Mike said. "It was visible in the daytime sky for three weeks and in the nighttime sky for two years." He went on to explain some historic Pueblo astronomical beliefs and their ancient connections.

"Certainly Pueblos are Anasazi descendants. It's not hard to make the hypothesis that the Anasazi operated in pretty much the same way as Pueblo Indians. Some beliefs have disappeared, some have changed, but in some ways you feel the underlying continuity of their religious life. So we can run the story backwards, but with caution.

"It's safe to say the Anasazi kept a calendar by sun watching and moon watching. They had people like Pueblo sun priests who were responsible for observing and forecasting for various planting cycles and religious ceremonies. The most important religious ceremony was probably held at the winter solstice. It marked the middle of the year, the turning around of the sun.

"In pueblos along the Rio Grande, the town chief, who's also the religious leader, does the sun watching and can be reprimanded by the two war chiefs if he doesn't get the forecasting right. The town chief represents the sun, and the war chiefs represent Venus as the morning and evening stars. They believe those stars are attached to the sun and never get far from it. The sun can be kept in line by the morning and evening stars, and so can their human representatives. This concept may have come from Mesoamerica.

"Observations were used for scheduling important ritual events. Forecasting allowed people to make proper ceremonial preparations—to get into the right frame of mind, practice songs and dances, assemble offerings and costumes. Otherwise, it would have been like having Easter without Lent, without warning. I have an idea that the sun priests in outlying villages miles north of Chaco watched the sun. They knew when it started rising at a certain place that in three or four days they'd have to leave for a ceremony in the canyon. Likewise, people miles away in another direction knew when it was time to go. You could have decentralized forecasting rather than people in Chaco deciding and then sending runners and signals.

"With the Hopi, some early corn is supposed to ripen enough to be used in summer-solstice ceremonies. The summer solstice is the last time you can plant corn here. Any later and it'll be killed by frost. Like their ancestors, they plant early, middle, and late corn and hope one crop will survive. They have multiple strategies to make sure they have adequate food supplies."

Careful observations, efficient forecasting, and required rituals could not prevent the prolonged drought that gripped Chaco Canyon from 1130 to 1180, and the subsequent collapse of the Chaco system. Large populations had used the environment to the point of exhaustion. Political, religious, and social organization began to fail. Trade with Mesoamerica ceased. Collectively, Chaco's town and village problems became those of a city in decline. Between about 1150 and 1200 most people moved on, probably abandoning the large towns first. Some Chacoans remained. Sporadically, Anasazi from Mesa Verde may have joined them, moving into old towns and villages or building small houses of their own. They remodeled some outlying towns and traded with the Mesa Verde heartland to the north.

The Mesa Verde Anasazi lived mostly in the high mesa country of southwestern Colorado and southeastern Utah. Like other Anasazi, they began moving from pit houses to aboveground pueblos between A.D. 700 and 900, building rooms and kivas on mesa tops and upland plains. By about 1000 they had become expert water and soil managers.

"Within Mesa Verde National Park alone, more than a thousand stone-check dams were built along the courses of ephemeral streams," says Linda Cordell. "These slowed the runoff of rain and snowmelt. The dams also trapped soil, so that the area behind these dams provided additional small garden plots."

On Chapin Mesa in the park, the stone-lined reservoir now called Mummy Lake measures about 90 feet in diameter. It was filled through a series of ditches, and some archaeologists think it served several nearby communities, attesting to cooperation among villages in work projects essential for survival.

Numerous small kivas mark Mesa Verde villages, suggesting to scholars that each served a clan, an extended family, or a small religious society. After about A.D. 1150 or 1200, the people began moving into large aggregated pueblos, just as other groups in the Southwest did. Many of these are the famed Mesa Verde cliff dwellings nestled inside rock-shelters, although some villages sit in open locations as well. Cliff dwellings range in size from one room to the estimated 220 rooms and 23 kivas of Cliff Palace. Distinct suites probably sheltered single households.

Writing about the mysterious two- and three-story towers common to Mesa Verde sites, Dr. Cordell notes that they often are connected to kivas by tunnels. "Most scholars have been intrigued by suggestions that the towers served either as defensive lookouts or as astronomical observatories. . . . Others suggest that, because the towers are often connected to kivas, their form may be purely religious and symbolic. They might, for example, represent mountains—the source of rainclouds and a symbol found in wall paintings of some Mesa Verde kivas."

But rainfall and environment failed. By A.D. 1300 Mesa Verde lay abandoned. Scholars believe the people of Mesa Verde eventually joined other Anasazi along the upper Rio Grande, where their descendants live today. (Continued on page 108)

Time-worn walls of Long House front a cliffside shelter in Colorado's Mesa Verde National Park. At right, coils stitched together with pliable splints shape a centuries-old willow basket found at the site. Pottery reduced the need for basketry among the Anasazi.

BASKET, DIAMETER C. 15¾ INCHES

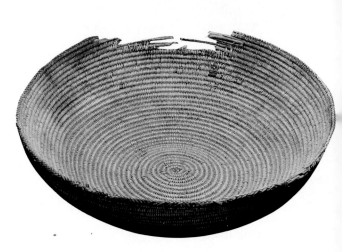

Light and shadow play over boldly patterned Mesa Verde pottery. Anasazi women often covered such coiled ware with a slip of clay, then painted and polished the surface before firing. Stylistic traditions and variations of black-on-white ceramics distinguished regional Anasazi groups.

Continuously occupied since the late 12th century, Acoma Pueblo crowns a mesa west of Albuquerque, New Mexico. Today's residents preserve ancient traditions and crafts. Potter Rebecca Lucario tempers her clay with ground sherds and shapes it in the way of her ancestors.

FOLLOWING PAGES: *Kayenta cliff dwelling of Keet Seel nestles below a streaked overhang in Arizona's Navajo National Monument.*

From about A.D. 500 to 1200, another Anasazi people, the Kayenta, lived in relatively small, scattered villages in northern Arizona and southern Utah. Compared to Chacoans, the Kayenta produced rather indifferent architecture, and they built fewer kivas than the people of Mesa Verde. But they excelled in handicrafts: Potters fashioned well-made bowls and jars, and painted them with geometric patterns; weavers produced brocade, tapestry, and tie-dyed fabrics with complex designs.

Around A.D. 1250, the Kayenta began building large cliff dwellings. The best known of these are Betatakin and Keet Seel, now preserved in Arizona's Navajo National Monument. Why did they choose to live in cliff dwellings rather than in open sites? Perhaps they wanted to use the canyon floors entirely for farming. Then, too, cliff dwellings offered protection from the elements and were ideal for storing food. At least one—Betatakin—contained a spring that provided drinking water. And because they were remote and hard to reach, cliff dwellings also had certain defensive advantages.

The defensive nature of some Kayenta sites is of special interest to archaeologist Jonathan Haas of the School of American Research in Santa Fe, New Mexico. "In valleys and canyons and on mesas I find evidence of conflict by about 1200," he told me. "Cycles of drought began years before. People were beginning to worry about what was happening. They had less arable land, and it continued to erode. The water table had dropped. Across a huge area, thousands of people started moving into major defensible locations, such as a mesa top 700 feet high. And villages got much bigger. Archaeologically speaking, it happened overnight.

"In 1250 in Arizona's Long House Valley you have five focal sites—big, defensible pueblos all located on hilltops surrounded by satellite sites. The really interesting thing is they are visually linked to one another. You can see this developing into a real system as opposed to little isolated villages. We ran a computer program with maps and asked which points in that valley are defensible and what the visibility is. We also located ten big, new focal sites in Kayenta Valley that turned out to be visually hooked up with the Long House system. One butte looked intuitively good on a map. I found a narrow crack that leads up the back of it, the only way up, and there was a 200-room pueblo on top! I found handholds and toeholds that link up cliff dwellings. They go up and over the canyon walls. More people than anybody ever imagined lived in this area."

We talked about the Kayenta cliff dwellings in Navajo National Monument. "When you go to Keet Seel," Jonathan said, "ask yourself why there was a big occupation moving in about 1250. Imagine attacking Keet Seel. Imagine seven small children trying to keep you out and then tell me who'd win. Form your own opinion."

Photographer Rik Cooke, his wife, Bronwyn, park ranger

Within village-like Keet Seel, a walkway or "street"—rare in cliff dwellings—winds past living quarters, storage chambers, and circular kivas. Several household groups occupied clusters of rooms. At left, a smoke hole pierces the mud-covered roof of a living room; beside it, an exposed roof reveals sticks and matting laid across beams.

BRONWYN A. COOKE (LEFT)

Mark Sterkel, two Navajo wranglers, and I set out for Keet Seel from a mesa top. We led our mounts and pack horses down a narrow trail sometimes notched into the 1,000-foot mesa face and onto the floor of the Tsegi Canyon system. We rode for eight miles—up and down steep, sandy gullies, around quicksand, and partway in a shallow stream. The horses tore off bites of sage as we went along, and sage perfumed one red-and-gold canyon we entered. Finally, we stood below Keet Seel, protected in its natural rock-shelter. Mark wired several wooden ladders together to span the 40-foot cliff face—and I began my assault.

I had ample time to form my own opinion about Keet Seel's defensibility. Terrified, I had time to study the color and texture of the rock, to memorize each pattern in the grain of the wooden ladders. I paused to ponder wire knots. My vertical onslaught came in fractions of inches. I formed an opinion: One toddler with a long-stemmed lily could have held me at bay.

Inside, the settlement revealed living quarters, storage rooms, kivas, streets. Sherds of polychrome pottery lay strewn about. It was as if the people had hoped to return. Some rooms had been carefully sealed. A cache of hundreds of small ears of corn remained in place. Wooden roofs still covered some rooms. In that dry, preserving air of the Southwest, it seemed as if we had missed the Anasazi's departure by only a matter of days.

"It must have been a rough period," Jonathan Haas had said. "It was hard on them agriculturally. They responded the way farmers still do, by overexploiting the land. They reached the point where they couldn't grow anything. They had run the game out. Skeletal material shows malnutrition. They were defending their towns—I think from other Anasazi, people from Mesa Verde, for example."

Sustaining water and the loss of it; arable land and the lack of it—by 1300 the Kayenta Anasazi had abandoned their large towns. Like their kinsmen at Chaco and Mesa Verde, they sought a more promising environment elsewhere.

A Zuni myth, recorded at the close of the 19th century, tells of the abandonment of Anasazi cliff dwellings. A giant called Cloud-swallower devoured men and consumed "the cloud-breaths of the beloved gods, and souls of the dead, whence descend rains . . . snow ceased in the north and the west; rain ceased in the south and the east; the mists of the mountains above were drunk up; the waters of the valleys below were dried up. . . ." Other supernaturals, the Twin Gods of War and Grandmother Spider, destroyed the dread swallower of clouds. "But fearing that never again would the waters refreshen their cañons, our ancients who dwelt in the cliffs fled away to the southward and eastward—all save those who had perished aforetime; they are dead in their homes in the cliff-towns, dried, like their cornstalks that died when the rain stopped long, long ago, when all things were new."

■

110

Gulf of Mexico

TULA●

●TEOTIHUACAN

●TENOCHTITLAN

Area enlarged

LA VENTA●

SAN LORENZO●

LAS LIMAS●

●MONTE ALBAN

M E X I C O

Pacific Ocean

Valley of Mexico

0 ——— 15 km
0 ——— 15 mi

L. Zumpango

L. Xaltocan

●TEOTIHUACAN

SANTA CECILIA
ACATITLAN●

*Lake
Texcoco*

AZCAPOTZALCO●

●TEXCOCO

●TLATELOLCO

TENOCHTITLAN

CHAPULTEPEC●

Dike

CULHUACAN●

L. Xochimilco

L. Chalco

MIXQUIC●

0 ——— 100 km
0 ——— 100 mi

Cape Catoche

IZAMAL

CHICHEN ITZA

MAYAPAN

COBA

Cozumel
Island

UXMAL
KABAH
JAINA
SAYIL
LABNA

TULUM

YUCATAN

PENINSULA

Ascension Bay

Caribbean Sea

CERROS

CALAKMUL

EL MIRADOR

UAXACTUN

PALENQUE

TIKAL

BELIZE

Bay Islands

BONAMPAK

*Gulf of
Honduras*

GUATEMALA

QUIRIGUA

IZAPA

COPAN

HONDURAS

KAMINALJUYU

EL SALVADOR

NICARAGUA

The maps locate sites in Mesoamerica referred to in this book.

A Golden Age in

MESOAMERICA

Kings were suns and gods on earth, ruling within great magical cycles of time. . . .

Incised stone mask depicts an Olmec ruler, who may have worn it in death. A shadowy people of obscure origin, the Olmecs flourished from about 1200 to 400 B.C. in southern Mexico and along the Pacific coast of Guatemala—and created Mesoamerica's first great art style.

Land and sea meet in shifting configurations along the southernmost shores of the Gulf of Mexico. There, in the present-day Mexican states of Veracruz and Tabasco, broad, sluggish rivers rise and fall with the tides, as do waters of marshlands where languid wading birds stride. Lakes and ponds dot a coastal plain webbed with streams. Swamps, exclusively neither land nor water, conceal stealthy reptiles and embrace islands where jaguars once prowled.

In winter, frequent storms bring deluge, drizzle, and mist. From late May through November, seasonal rains fall, broad savannas flood, and swollen rivers layer their natural levees with rich mud in a cycle of renewal not unlike that of the Nile. The alluvial riverbanks are the most productive lands in Mexico, and farmers grow corn and other crops year round.

This fertile coast was once the homeland of the Olmecs, an enigmatic people who developed the continent's first civilization. They were ruled by an elite obsessed with the worship of ancestors and the deified powers of nature. The central theme of their mysterious religion was the were-jaguar, a combination of man and jaguar, which they portrayed in jade figurines and on ornaments, pottery, and monuments. To honor powerful rulers and nurturing gods, they created the first great art style of the region anthropologists call Mesoamerica, which stretches from northern Mexico through Costa Rica. All the great Mesoamerican cultures that followed were heirs to the Olmec patrimony.

Around 2000 B.C., improved varieties of corn and other crops were cultivated, productivity increased, and populations expanded in Mesoamerica. By 1500 B.C. many farmers lived in hamlets, villages, and towns during a period of burgeoning civilization scholars call Preclassic or Formative.

Beginning about 1200 B.C., San Lorenzo, an Olmec town lying on a branch of the Coatzalcoalcos River, developed into Mesoamerica's earliest known religious and political center. Its people did not live by crops alone; evidence shows they consumed large amounts of fish and dog meat—and ate human captives. While scholars hesitate to call San Lorenzo a city in the strictest sense, it probably dominated two settlements nearby and perhaps ruled a vast adjoining area.

San Lorenzo lay atop a plateau that rises 164 feet above the surrounding countryside and can be seen for miles around. Manmade ravines and ridges jutted from three sides of it. The enormous construction, including a 23-foot layer of earth on top, contained tens of thousands of cubic yards of fill, clay, and sand, all carried there by workers, for ancient North Americans had neither beasts of burden nor wheeled conveyances. Archaeologist Michael D. Coe of Yale University, who excavated the site in the 1960s, believes that "the entire plateau is some kind of effigy mound, perhaps a gigantic bird flying east, but that the plan was never completed."

Colossal basalt head unearthed at San Lorenzo portrays an Olmec ruler. Pitted, then buried by unknown destroyers around 900 B.C., the sculpture stands more than 9 feet high and weighs more than 20 tons.

The site includes some 200 mounds, most of them the remains of dwellings. Other house mounds stretch into the distance. San Lorenzo itself had perhaps a thousand inhabitants. Mexican archaeologist Ignacio Bernal estimates that some 350,000 people may have occupied the Olmec heartland.

The large mounds at San Lorenzo must have been ceremonial structures. Courtyards flanked a central pyramid, and one enclosure likely marks Mesoamerica's earliest known ball court; clay figurines found at the site depict ball players in sacred-sport regalia. Pools constructed within the center probably were used for ritual bathing. At least one stone aqueduct system drew water from a ceremonial lake—the earliest form of water control known in North America. The nearest source of basalt for the U-shaped drains lay in the Tuxtla Mountains, more than 40 miles away.

From basalt, too, the Olmecs carved colossal portrait heads of their rulers. At least eight of them stood at San Lorenzo. To lessen the weight of the boulders, sculptors probably completed the carvings at the base of the Tuxtla range. "The technical expertise required to get these stones from their source to the San Lorenzo plateau must have been mind-boggling," Dr. Coe told me.

118

"They must have been dragged down to the nearest navigable stream or river, loaded on very large rafts, and perhaps even floated out to sea before being poled up the Coatzalcoalcos. Monuments weighing in some cases more than 20 tons were probably pulled uphill on rollers. Almost certainly this involved the forced labor of hundreds or perhaps even thousands of people."

A network of trade and procurement spread across Mesoamerica, supplying the Olmec elite with raw materials. As much as a ton of obsidian, the steel of ancient Mesoamerican technology, came from the highlands of Mexico and Guatemala to San Lorenzo. Artisans in workshops fashioned imported materials into products—flint tools, objects of serpentine and mica, and polished iron-ore beads, earspools, and mirrors used in divination. What did the Olmecs send out in return? Possibly textiles, exotic plumes, sacred books, and wooden religious items sought for prestige and ceremony by distant groups who looked to the Olmecs as cultural and religious models. Certainly they exported small stone carvings and pottery marked with icons; Olmec objects have been discovered all over Mesoamerica and were often treasured as sacred antiquities by later cultures.

Around 900 B.C. chaos engulfed San Lorenzo. It did not collapse slowly as most cities do, but instead fell victim to iconoclastic fury. Was it an invasion, a rebellion, or a large-scale ritual? Since the Olmecs left no written records, we shall probably never know. Incredibly, mobs worked as hard to demolish massive

Attended by dwarfs, an Olmec ruler surveys his likeness in stone as workers prepare to pull it into San Lorenzo. Stonecutters probably quarried and shaped such huge basalt heads in the Tuxtla Mountains, more than 40 miles away. Legions of laborers hauled them on log rollers overland to the Coatzalcoalcos River and floated them on rafts downstream to San Lorenzo. Ancient Mesoamericans achieved such feats without wheels, metal tools, or beasts of burden.

stone monuments as artisans had to carve them. The destroyers dragged thrones and sculptures from their original positions, placed them in lines, and fractured, slotted, pounded, pitted, and then buried them. San Lorenzo never recovered, although smaller populations continued living there for centuries.

A man-made clay mound with fluted sides rises from a swamp-encircled island sanctuary near the Tonala River to dominate La Venta, a site first occupied about 1100 B.C. and probably the political and ceremonial successor to San Lorenzo. The mound took perhaps 800,000 man-days to complete, and after centuries of erosion it still stands about a hundred feet high. Perhaps a representation of a distant sacred volcano, the mound is part of the earliest known platform pyramid, a construction that endured in ancient Mesoamerica and served to raise shrines and temples high above ceremonial plazas.

La Venta was a ceremonial center in the strictest sense, and it reveals the Mesoamerican concern for sacred landscape. In a configuration that may represent a massive were-jaguar mask, the site lies eight degrees west of north, aligned astronomically with the heavens of 3,000 years ago. Smaller structures stretched in bilateral symmetry beyond the mound. By this time the Olmecs had sources of jade, the ancient Mesoamerican symbol of wealth, and La Venta people buried offerings of jade celts and

Cross-legged beneath an altar or a throne, an Olmec ruler of La Venta grasps a cord. Sign of supremacy, it binds captives carved on the sides of the massive stone. Most sculptural motifs at Mesoamerican sites emphasize royal authority and status.

5¼ FEET HIGH

Sculpted in greenstone, a youth cradles an infant with the stylized jaguar eyes and mouth of the Olmec rain deity. Faces engraved on the knees, shoulders, and face of the larger figure represent other gods in the Olmec pantheon. Two children at play in Las Limas in the Mexican state of Veracruz discovered the 22-inch-high statue in 1965.

figurines and iron-ore mirrors in the plaza. They outlined royal tombs with large basalt columns. They created three mosaic pavements of were-jaguar masks from serpentine slabs and ceremonially covered them on completion. Their efforts were not destined to last, however, for La Venta's end, too, was marked by the cataclysmic destruction of colossal heads, thrones, and other monuments. The center collapsed by 400 B.C.

The basic Mesoamerican settlement pattern that generally prevailed until the Spanish conquest had been established. Rulers, priests, and their retainers lived in elite centers. Surrounding hamlets and villages supplied labor to build and maintain palaces and temples, and provided food for the residents. Markets held in the centers redistributed food and manufactured goods.

Populations multiplied, and, in the centers that dotted the Mesoamerican landscape, regional art and architecture flourished. A 260-day ritual calendar and a 365-day solar calendar came into wide use; the Olmecs probably developed both of them. A system of bars and dots was used to express numbers.

"Along with the elaborate ritual and solar calendars," said Dr. Coe, "hieroglyphic writing sprang up early to ensure the accurate recording of time and to celebrate great events in the life of the elite."

The great center of Kaminaljuyu on the outskirts of present-day Guatemala City reached its maximum extent by 500 B.C. and had a long and influential history. Izapa, on Guatemala's Pacific slopes, and Tikal and El Mirador in the lowlands also developed into important centers. But perhaps Monte Alban, in the Mexican state of Oaxaca, illustrates the development of Preclassic states most dramatically. The city was the capital of the Zapotecs, and it stood on a 1,311-foot hill that rises abruptly where three arms of the Oaxaca Valley merge.

Some of the earliest writing in the New World appeared at Monte Alban. Certainly the first true literary texts have been found there. Those hieroglyphs carved on stone slabs tell of the city's rise to glory. Some 140 slabs show men in contorted postures, with open mouths and closed eyes; several bleed, some are mutilated, and one is nothing more than a severed head. They are the corpses of slain enemy chiefs or kings. Accompanying glyphs surely record their names and the dates of their deaths, although many of them remain undeciphered.

"This obsession with recording victories over enemies characterizes early civilizations the world over, and the rising Preclassic states of Mexico were no exception," Dr. Coe told me. "It speaks for a time when polities were relatively small and engaged in mutual warfare, when no ruler could extend his sway over a territory large enough to be called an empire."

As early as 500 B.C., Monte Alban had conquered most rival valley towns and become the area's regional capital. Some 5,000 people, about half the valley's population, came to live on residential terraces built along the high slopes. Laborers leveled the uppermost reaches of the hill, creating a platform 820 yards long and 273 yards wide for religious and civic buildings. This primary center administered an area extending some four miles around the site; secondary centers, with an average population of about 200 each, served as administrative head towns for districts. Villages and hamlets of fewer than 150 people dotted the valley. Populations increased, and so did the need for control, regularization, labor, and farmland. Zapotecs practiced irrigation, drawing water from mountain springs to terraced fields through canals. By 300 to 200 B.C., some 30,000 people lived in one arm of the valley alone, and 10,000 to 20,000 in the city itself.

Monte Alban had carved out for itself a time of peace, of efficient farming, organized administration, and prosperity that endured in part because of the city's isolation from other great powers. During the Classic period, which began by A.D. 150 except in the Maya area, Monte Alban housed perhaps 24,000 people. Subject populations may have numbered in the hundreds of thousands. Towns, villages, hamlets, and irrigation canals blanketed the valley floor in an ancient version of urban sprawl.

Silent above Mexico's Oaxaca Valley, ruined temples and pyramids around a plaza recall the greatness of Monte Alban. People known as the Zapotecs flattened a lofty hilltop to build their capital, which by the sixth century A.D. had burgeoned into a city-state with perhaps 60,000 inhabitants.

Enigmatic effigy in an elaborate headdress gazes from a funerary urn found at Monte Alban. At right, figures popularly called the "Danzantes," or Dancers, crouch in low relief on huge stone slabs—some of about 140 that possibly adorned a kind of war memorial. With their contorted limbs, gaping mouths, and closed eyes, the carvings represent corpses, perhaps of enemies slain by rulers of the city.

Architecture in the capital included masonry buildings, a ball court, and 170 known tombs of wealthy kings and other elite. Funerary urns portraying gods accompanied the elite in death; gods process in murals along tomb walls. Monte Alban shared deities with Teotihuacan, a formidable power to the north, as well as with other highland centers; among them were the rain god and the feathered serpent, a water deity. The lofty capital

collapsed at about the same time Teotihuacan did, around A.D. 700, probably because of far-reaching economic failure.

Cultures of the Classic period in Mesoamerica reached a mature sophistication based on vibrant concepts developed in Preclassic days. The Classic period became Mesoamerica's golden age, a time of intellectual and artistic achievement unmatched before or after. It was a time of literacy in a land of magic.

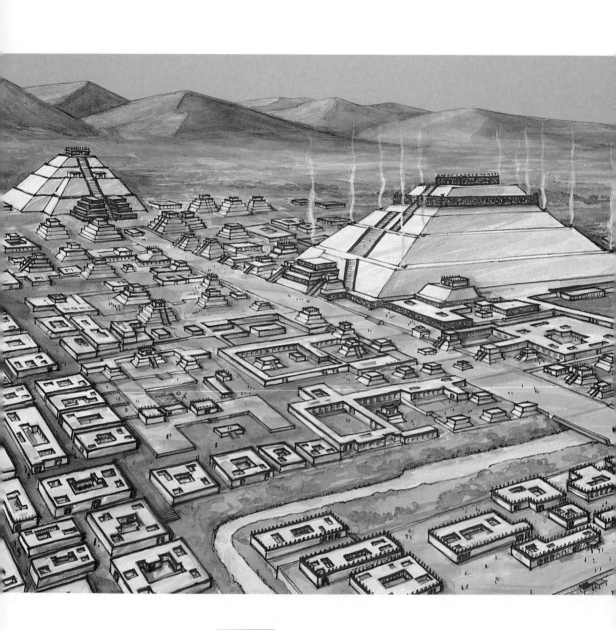

Teotihuacan. The very name means "Place of the Gods." Its valley is part of the larger Valley of Mexico, and the last great Aztec emperor, Moctezuma II, made pilgrimages there on foot to visit shrines and honor ancient deities. To the Aztecs the city was a mythical and sacred place. There, they said, time began and the sun and moon were born. There the first people emerged from a hidden cave.

The Aztecs called the largest structure in Teotihuacan the Pyramid of the Sun, and that probably was its original name, for it faces the setting sun at zenith. It is also the city's earliest monumental structure, built over an ancient ceremonial cave that was probably viewed as the supernatural place of emergence. In this

North America's first planned city, Teotihuacan at its height in
A.D. 500 spreads over an area of eight square miles in the Valley of
Mexico. Builders continued to follow a grid system established some
five centuries earlier, even channeling a river to conform to it. The
three-mile-long Street of the Dead links the Pyramid of the Moon (far
left) with the Citadel and its Temple of Quetzalcoatl (far right). Along
the avenue the massive Pyramid of the Sun towers more than 200 feet.
A market (foreground) occupies the courtyard of the Compound.
Streets subdivide the metropolis into districts with specialized
workshops, and apartment compounds housing as many as 200,000.
ART BY DENNIS SIMON

sacred place the city was born about 100 B.C., developing from one of the many villages that dotted the valley. By the beginning of the Christian era the Pyramid of the Sun was complete, rising some 200 feet high, with a base measuring 728 by 738 feet. It covers an area almost as large as that of the Pyramid of Cheops in Egypt, and it remained one of the largest structures in North America until the 20th century. A structure begun soon afterward, the Pyramid of the Moon, is smaller but more complex. An extinct volcano, strikingly similar in shape, frames it to the north, and a comparable mountain lies to the south. To Mesoamericans, pyramids symbolized mountains in a sacred landscape.

Dazzling in sunlight, the Pyramid of the Moon climbs more than 130 feet in a series of five terraces. Powerful rulers, strangely anonymous, had Teotihuacan's immense structures built to glorify the gods. Above, a stone serpent head thrusts from the facade of the Temple of Quetzalcoatl—Feathered Serpent—one of the city's supreme deities.

FOLLOWING PAGES: *The Pyramid of the Moon complex displays the city's architectural hallmark, the* talud-tablero *style—sloping bases supporting parallel tiers. Time has erased most of the painted stucco that once covered the tableros, like giant murals within stone frames.*

"In Teotihuacan, with the great pyramids completed, a gigantic urban plan began to emerge," archaeologist Doris Heyden told me in Mexico. "It reflected their ideas about astronomy and their desire to truly identify with the serene landscape of the Mexican plateau."

Teotihuacan was North America's first planned city, and its builders evidently kept to the original plan through the centuries as the city grew. Streets and most buildings followed a grid aligned with the city center, the whole oriented some 15 degrees east of north. The basic unit of measurement, about 57 meters (187 feet), determined the size of most residential units, and

In the patio of an elite residence, the wife of a Teotihuacan lord instructs one of her daughters in the art of weaving while other children play nearby. Families lived in apartment compounds— single-story dwellings within high stone enclosures. Murals such as the reconstructed ones at right often brightened patio and portico walls.

many streets repeat multiples of the 57-meter scale. An avenue called the Street of the Dead forms the north-south axis, running south from the Pyramid of the Moon for more than three miles. Another axis runs east and west; together, they divide the city into quadrants. Avenues run parallel to the north-south axis at regular intervals. Builders even channeled the San Juan River, which ran through the city, to conform to the grid.

In the second and third centuries architectural complexes rose along the axes—the ceremonial heart of the city. A building in the complex called the Citadel, at the intersection, probably served as a palace in the early years, thus placing the rulers at the center of the four sacred directions, at the center of the universe. Over time, the Citadel was enlarged to include platforms, temples, residences, and a courtyard of nearly 11 acres that could hold 100,000 people. The Temple of Quetzalcoatl at its center has sculptured feathered serpents, symbolizing water and fertility, that alternate with fire serpents, symbolizing hot, barren land— the kind of duality often expressed by Mesoamericans. An even larger complex, the Compound, sat across the avenue from the Citadel and may have served as a marketplace. This majestic core area had become a religious and political precinct, the power center of the Teotihuacan state, and the residence of some 250 to 400 elite individuals and thousands of their retainers.

Teotihuacan was the most highly urbanized center of its

FOLLOWING PAGES: Resplendent in a feather headdress, a Maya ruler prepares to address the crowd below the Danta Pyramid in El Mirador. Around and beyond the 43-acre plaza rise other ceremonial and civic buildings. Established in present-day Guatemala about 150 B.C., the city thrived as a political and economic seat, but was mysteriously abandoned two centuries later.

time in the entire New World, and in size and splendor it surpassed Old World cities of later times. At the height of its power, around A.D. 500, it covered eight square miles, an area larger than imperial Rome. Some archaeologists estimate that 125,000 people lived in Teotihuacan; others say the residential population may have exceeded 200,000.

More than 4,000 structures, most of them single-story apartment buildings, housed the population. As many as a hundred people related by kinship, profession, or both lived in each building. Each apartment had its own rooms and shrines, and usually an enclosed patio. The city was subdivided into neighborhoods, at least one of which included foreign residents; Zapotec merchants or artisans lived there for generations. More than 600 workshops—400 for obsidian, 200 for ceramics—dotted the city.

To the modern visitor, temples, pyramids, and other structures along the Street of the Dead give an impression of overpowering mass. Giants or the gods themselves, said the Aztecs, must have built them. Tens of thousands of visitors at the site today could never evoke the pomp and splendor of residents, emissaries, merchants, and pilgrims milling about the ancient city of stuccoed and brightly painted buildings. People adorned in jewelry, colorful fabrics, and plumes must have hoped to glimpse priests and other members of the ruling classes wearing even more elaborate jewelry, garments, and headdresses.

Murals depict gods in the guise of animals or humans in elaborate regalia. The Teotihuacan pantheon included Tlaloc, the rain god; his consort, a water goddess; the old fire god; Quetzalcoatl, the plumed serpent; and gods of commerce, the morning

Potsherds spread on a screen intrigue graduate student Ellen Stutz Landeen, who discovered them in an elite residence at El Mirador in 1982. A colleague, Richard Hansen (opposite), cleans one of the large stucco masks on the Tigre Temple. They combine symbols of royalty that appear in later Maya iconography.

star, flowers, and death. Later art shows militaristic figures in battle array. No inscriptions in art or architecture record rulers or historical facts, nor do any painted books survive.

Was the Teotihuacan state a military empire, or one of trade, or both? Scholars prefer to speak of a "Teotihuacan presence" throughout Mesoamerica. The city's influence was powerful and widespread. Painted vessels from Teotihuacan adorned tombs of distant kings. Kaminaljuyu, some 700 miles away, became a copy of the larger city. Monte Alban, too, was closely linked with the capital. Teotihuacan may have dominated obsidian mining and its profitable trade throughout Mesoamerica.

About A.D. 600 Teotihuacan's power began to slip. The city had developed in an area of springs, and a vast irrigation and chinampa, or island garden, system had helped provide abundant food. But a climatic change occurred that had devastating effects. Overplanting in other areas may have exhausted fields. Widespread deforestation created long-term erosion. Skeletal studies show a prevalence of ravaging disease. Less sophisticated groups to the north became restless and may have exerted pressure. The population endured great stress for a century. There is some evidence that the heart of the city went up in flames about A.D. 700, during an invasion, a rebellion, or both.

The lords of Teotihuacan may have managed to escape, but no doubt other inhabitants stayed on. "You can have a situation where a city loses its trade empire and is vastly diminished in size, and is unable to sustain the level of affluence it had before, but still a fair number of people can live off whatever remains in the economy," archaeologist Susan Evans of Pennsylvania State

Caressing couple— young goddess, old god—steps out of the Maya's golden age. From about A.D. 600 to 900 the Maya mass- produced such fired-clay figurines; many have been found in graves on Jaina Island off Yucatan. From them scholars gain knowledge of Classic Maya dress, ornaments, and customs.

C. 10 INCHES HIGH, © 1987
THE DETROIT INSTITUTE OF ARTS

University told me. "Population estimates show that after its fall Teotihuacan was one-third to one-fifth of its former size, so it still had maybe 30,000 people, and that's still a really big Mesoameri- can city. I like to compare it to Beirut, which was the Paris of the Mediterranean 20 years ago. Now it doesn't sustain a lot of com- mercial activity or tourism. People don't swarm there to live. But it does function, and people do live there."

The downfall of the sacred place where the sun was born and time began marked the end of the Classic period in Mexico's central highlands. Teotihuacan took other glorious centers down with it. British archaeologist Nigel Davies comments that the "fall of Teotihuacan, like that of Rome, three centuries before, left in its wake a disordered world, whose surviving cities were like planets in orbit round an extinct sun."

During the Preclassic period in the Maya lowlands, the sun god had appeared boldly on earth, and Maya kings became his incarnations. From the center of the cosmos they interceded between their subjects and the supernaturals, and great cycles of time and the universe—the sources of human power—coursed around them.

The god's manifestation happened quickly, considering the long span of archaeological time. A slow rise in population and development had marked the first millennium B.C., and by 300 B.C. a more complex social and political organization had arisen. In many lowland areas, intensive agriculture and major water- management programs maintained a greatly increased popula- tion. About 50 B.C., in a burst of construction and iconographic expression, centers in the lowlands had an unprecedented flo- rescence. At Cerros in present-day Belize, El Mirador in Guate- mala, and other sites, massive stucco masks representing the face of the sun flanked balustrades on lofty pyramids.

The Preclassic center of El Mirador thrived from about 150 B.C. to A.D. 150 and was probably a city-state from early times. It was certainly a city of startling proportions. The base of one pyra- mid, El Tigre, covers more than 20,000 square yards—the size of three football fields. Including the structures on top, it soars to a height of 18 stories. With its associated platforms and buildings, the complex measures about 70,000 square yards—larger than the base of the Pyramid of the Sun at Teotihuacan. Archaeologist Ray T. Matheny of Brigham Young University describes the site as having a "ceremonial layout, a host of elite residences, reser- voirs, causeways, a precinct wall, and public building construc- tion that rivals in size anything ever built by the Maya in either the Lowlands or Highlands during any period."

Why did the Maya abandon the city? There are no written rec- ords to offer clues, and since most of the site remains shrouded in tropical forest, excavations have not yet provided an answer.

138

Many centers continued, developing into city-states that reached their height during the Classic Maya period. That period began about A.D. 250, when the Maya brought an accurate calendar system called the long count into use. Glyphs developed to a point where the Maya could express themselves completely. Their writing system surpassed all others in the New World.

The Classic Maya was a glorious period of art and scholarship, of political and religious fervor. Stars in alignment summoned men to battle, and kings reigned by the unquestioned mandate of myths. Kings were suns and gods on earth, ruling within great magical cycles of time at the center of the cosmos.

The Maya cosmos included an earth of four quarters within a multilayered universe. It had, writes archaeologist Wendy Ashmore of Rutgers University, "a many-tiered heaven above, wherein the ancestors reside, and a similarly stratified underworld, the home of various other supernaturals, and the scene of primordial ordeals involving the legendary Hero Twins...." The sun, moon, Venus, and other deities moved in cycles through the upper world and the underworld. In a Maya myth, the Hero Twins descend to the underworld, endure trials, are sacrificed, but miraculously live again and rise triumphant. Originally the pair were the sun and Venus; in later versions they became the sun and the moon.

The Maya believed that mountains mediated between earth and sky, and caves linked the earth with the underworld. Pyramids symbolized mountains, and temple doorways, caves. Thus architecture and city planning were actually metaphorical maps of a complex belief system. Rulers performed essential ceremonies, often ones of self-sacrifice. They pierced themselves and offered their blood. Since blood is the life force, the ritual nurtured the gods themselves, who in turn nourished the Maya people.

Kings used art, architecture, and inscriptions to proclaim their royal and divine heritage. Maya inscriptions have been

Vase paintings open windows on the Maya world. This one, shown in a rollout photograph, records a bloodletting ceremony at a Maya court. Seated on a platform, the ruler holds a flowerlike lancet; a dwarf props up a mirror. Maya royalty pierced themselves to sanctify major events—the birth of an heir, the dedication of a temple—or to intercede with the gods on behalf of the people.
© JUSTIN KERR 1987

likened to billboards, for they were masterstrokes of advertising and public relations. In sensational glyphic headlines they proclaimed political accomplishments, divinity, ancestry, and, therefore, the right to rule. As bold as flashing neon, inscribed monuments never stopped reminding passersby of preordained absolute power.

Modern visitors can almost hear as well as see the vivid events portrayed in murals at Bonampak in southern Mexico. The paintings, intended to be viewed in sequence, begin with nobles honoring a child in arms, presented as heir to the throne. Another mural shows a celebration honoring the child. Musicians play as costumed figures perform. The scene changes: Amid spears, shields, and the dead and dying, warriors in a furious battle win a Bonampak victory over a neighboring city. The next scene shows tortured captives marked for sacrifice cowering in agony and humiliation on a stairway. The haughty king, Chan Muan, and his royal court stand at the top, dressed in jaguar skins, jade, quetzal plumes, and animal-shaped headdresses. In the final mural, constellation signs and a date seem to record Venus rising as the morning star on August 2 in A.D. 792. That dawn must have been an auspicious or foreboding one requiring appropriate sacrifice, for the captives meet their death on a pyramid, and the royal family, including the child, pierce their tongues with spines or draw ropes through them to offer blood.

Splendors of Maya court life unfold in a reproduction of temple murals from Bonampak in Mexico. Musicians with gourd rattles, drums, and turtle shell instruments march across the lower panel in a procession honoring the child heir to the throne; lords of the city fill the panels above. Discovered in 1946, the original polychrome murals rank as the finest known examples of Classic Maya wall painting.

FLORIDA STATE MUSEUM

Warfare, as the Bonampak murals attest, marked the era of glorious city-states as a time when political boundaries fluctuated and polities flourished, failed, and sometimes rose again. Royal prestige rather than economic gain became the goal of war. An estimated 22 independent polities controlled the southern Maya lowlands about A.D. 790. But nowhere is the story of a Classic polity more dramatic or complete than at the southernmost known Maya city, Copan, in the mountains of western Honduras. It was lifted to greatness by 16 kings in a single dynasty.

April desiccates the narrow Copan Valley, which stretches along the Copan River for some eight miles. It is the height of the dry season. Cattle appear to plod along paths on cushions of dust, and grass seems brittle beyond rejuvenation. A haze settles over the mountains and weighs upon the sun-baked valley. Daily rains will not bring the landscape to life for almost two months. It was in April that I first visited Copan.

I toured the site with archaeologist William Fash of Northern Illinois University, who heads the Copan Mosaics Project, an ongoing effort of excavation and restoration. We climbed steep pyramids and clambered over temples, then picked our way down inside a secluded courtyard to a rounded, carved stone scholars call Altar Q. The monument bears 16 sculpted figures, each

Now deserted, the ball court at Copan once resounded with shouts of spectators at games — part sport, part ritual — in which players moved a hard rubber ball, soccer-style, toward special markers. Southernmost of known Maya cities and among the largest, Copan (opposite) lies in a narrow valley in western Honduras.

sitting cross-legged on his glyphic name. These are the kings of Copan, and they form a closed circle that illustrates the story of the city. The kings turn to each other as if in conversation across the centuries. The last ruler looks at his neighbor, the first ruler of Copan, and accepts a gift. "He is receiving a badge of office, a right to rule, from the first king," said Bill. That first ancestor had ruled some 400 years before.

Experts, volunteers, students, and local laborers worked at the main site. Bill and I passed massive mounds of carved stones. "We have around 20,000 fragments of sculpture fallen from different temples," said Bill. "It's the largest jigsaw puzzle in Mesoamerica. What's worse, we don't even have the box top to look at! The biggest problem is what we call the GOK piles — the God-only-knows piles. We find pieces from maybe five or six buildings thrown in one heap by earlier archaeologists who figured it was an impossibility and gave up. But we've already put two temples together. The Maya wanted to make a statement

142

Expert interpreter of Maya glyphs and a student at Princeton University, David Stuart (above) examines symbols carved in stucco on an older structure beneath Copan's Temple 26 (opposite, in background). Rudi Larios, a native of Guatemala in charge of restoration for the Copan Mosaics Project, takes a look at a reconstructed mask on Temple 22.

with every temple, so no two are alike. We're working our way through the piles, understanding each temple individually."

Local laborers and American college students excavated near the Hieroglyphic Stairway of Temple 26. David Stuart—a student at Princeton, a glyph expert, and my youngest son—was among them. With 1,263 glyph blocks, the stairway bears the longest ancient inscription in the New World—and seven to ten steps are missing. It, too, is a jigsaw puzzle, for only glyphs on the lowest steps remain in their original order. Those higher up slumped and tumbled through the centuries, and earlier archaeologists put them back at a time when most glyphs had not been deciphered. With about 70 percent of the stones out of place, the long inscription of dynastic information makes little more sense than a jumbled alphabet rearranged by an illiterate.

Archaeologists have worked at Copan off and on for nearly a century; Bill has spent ten seasons there. Their findings, along with new glyphic interpretations, give a factual account rather than a mythical one of how a particular city came to be. As an unseasonable downpour began, Bill and I took shelter in a temple near the ball court, and he told me the story of Copan.

"The earliest house we've found in the valley dates from about 1100 B.C.," he began. "The first stirrings of complex culture came by about 600 B.C. People lived on a village level. Copan was a great place to be. The interesting thing is that everybody left the valley about 300 to 200 B.C., and it was a backwater again. Presumably more exciting things were going on at other sites. You

144

get this pulsation in the Maya area—cities booming for about 100 to 200 years and then going downhill in a hurry. This suggests charismatic rulers who offer incentives for people to settle in their city. Then when a weak ruler comes along, the system goes down, and everybody charges off to another city.

"After A.D. 400 things at Copan really started picking up. I think it was because of the first king, Yax Kuk Mo, or Resplendent Quetzal-Macaw, who came to power in 430. He was a mover and shaker who got things rolling. People started building ball courts and temple-pyramids and inscribing hieroglyphs. All subsequent rulers recognized him as the founder of their dynasty. He's the George Washington of Copan.

"At this site, macaws decorated ball courts, and that was true for 400 years. The macaw may have been the patron of the royal line, and it may refer to the name of the first king. David has read glyphs that indicate Macaw Mountain may have been the ancient name of Copan. That would tie everything together—geography, the city, and the kings.

"No more than 3,000 to 4,000 people lived here during Yax Kuk Mo's reign. Another charismatic ruler, Smoke Jaguar, the twelfth king, ruled late in the seventh century. He was the 'Great Instigator.' He consolidated boundaries and marked them with monuments that expressed power and sacred geography. With big influxes of people during his reign, the population shot up to as high as 10,000. People spread out and even farmed hill slopes.

"In the eighth century populations continued to go up. Copan probably ruled an area of nearly a hundred square miles. Early in the eighth century 18 Rabbit, the 'Great Integrator,' came to power. He built two causeways connecting the city's core with outlying settlements. He erected stelae—carved monuments showing himself in his glory—in the plaza designed for spectacular rituals. Sculptures became flamboyant and almost fully in the round. His reign may well have marked the culmination of sculpture and hieroglyphic writing at Copan.

"One of David's greatest discoveries this season is that 18 Rabbit built Temple 22 to commemorate the 20th anniversary of his reign. Now what did the king put on his temple? A giant benevolent cosmogram—all the symbols of the supernatural forces of the universe for the population to see; the two-headed sky band with Venus as one head and the sun as the other. The body, the arc of heaven, had smoke and blood intertwined with gods that the king brought forth. The king performed rites in the temple and then emerged as hundreds of people waited below for the divine word. From the number of monuments he erected we know he was a great ruler, and from their symbols and texts we can see he was a man of vision.

"But invaders came, and the king of Quirigua captured 18 Rabbit, took him to his city, and beheaded him. Now, Quirigua was just a piddling rival, and the execution made its king a

Beside an ornate stela bearing the figure of a ruler, project leader William Fash of Northern Illinois University describes ongoing restoration work at Copan. The leaf-nosed bat symbol (above)— the emblem glyph of Copan—probably stands for the polity centered in the ancient city; it appears on the monument just above the brim of Fash's hat.

ART BY BARBARA W. FASH

Royal story in stone on Copan's Altar Q recounts the transfer of power from one ruler to another within a single dynasty. A gigantic jigsaw puzzle, the Hieroglyphic Stairway (opposite) of Temple 26 contains 1,263 glyph blocks jumbled over the centuries. Guided by project artist Barbara Fash, who watches with foreman Ramón Guerra, David Stuart fits a block into its correct position.

charismatic ruler. He even claimed to be king of Copan. What happened in Copan after this humiliating defeat? The 15th king, Smoke Shell, built Temple 26 with its Hieroglyphic Stairway to reaffirm the glory of the royal lineage, and tried to reinvigorate the city by portraying the former kings as warriors with shields in one hand and spears in the other. Suddenly inscriptions are not talking about gods and sky and Venus and the sun. They're the voices of evil and warfare, with signs of the underworld and sacrifice on the temple. They say these kings are in control."

Only days before my arrival David had excavated beneath the altar at the foot of the Hieroglyphic Stairway and discovered a dedicatory treasure. The offering included a flint knife, eccentric flints bearing human profiles, and two jade sculptures that must have been centuries-old royal heirlooms when buried. Perhaps the most dramatic part of the offering was a closed spiny oyster shell: Stains inside indicate it probably held an offering of blood. "The cache was in keeping with the concept of the temple," said Bill. "Lineage, the right to rule, and royal blood."

A causeway leads from Copan's center to the settlement of a prestigious and wealthy family of scribes. Sculpture adorns the small palace there, and inscriptions honor the family. "I think it was a holy spot," said Bill. "Here we have the longest occupation in the valley—some 3,000 years." In such settlements the story of Copan's final years unfolded.

"Copan reached its apogee in the eighth century," said Bill.

Bloodletting ritual begins for Smoke Shell, the 15th ruler of Copan, as a royal attendant hands him a shell containing stingray spines. He will pierce his penis with them and let his blood flow into a bowl. The highly formalized ceremony takes place around A.D. 750 in the building now called Temple 22. Glyphs, skulls, human figures, and mythological creatures frame the entrance to the inner chamber.

Cache found in 1987 beneath the Hieroglyphic
Stairway yielded a wealth of ritual artifacts, most of
them placed in a covered clay pot. The shell holds
stingray spines and may contain dried blood. Three
flints carved with faces in profile may have served as
insignias of power. The jade plaque, bearing sun and
jaguar symbols, and the squat male effigy, also of jade,
passed as heirlooms through generations of rulers.

Wide double-columned doorways distinguish the palace of Sayil in the dry, hilly area of central Yucatan known as the Puuc. About A.D. 800, as Maya cities in the south began to decline, dozens of northern centers—Sayil, Labna, Uxmal, and Kabah among them— rose to prominence.

"The valley had about 12 elite settlements like this one. Then there were settlements of the upper middle and middle classes, both with their retainers, and many small peasant households. The valley had become very crowded by the last half of the century. The demand for wood meant total deforestation for a radius of perhaps 18 miles. This led to erosion and overuse of land. The pity of it is, if they had been conservative, the valley could have supported them. But without the forest a heat vacuum set in, and rainfall declined. Corn came in thinner every year. Studies of skeletal remains show that 90 percent of the population was seriously ill from malnutrition, disease, or both. Nine out of every ten people! Infant mortality skyrocketed. And along with the economic crunch came a political crunch."

The last king, known as Yax Pac, assumed power in 762. He proudly noted on monuments that his mother came from the royal family of Palenque, a great Maya city in Mexico. (Classic leaders often strengthened power through royal marriages.) Yax

152

Pac erected Temple 11, one of the grandest structures at Copan.
A monument shows him as a mighty warrior wearing a belt with
trophy heads of slain enemies dangling from it.

"He's saying, 'Don't mess with me.' If he has to show this,
it's basically a reflection of weakness," said Bill. "He's running
scared. He doesn't have support any more. The elite had literally
sucked the system dry. All Maya society was top-heavy in the
late Classic period. Elite landholders at Copan no longer provided tribute to the king. They said, 'Forget it, guy, we're diseased
and starving and have to take care of our own.' A lot of upstart
nobles declared themselves independent.

"There are also monuments dedicated by the king at the palaces and shrines of important families outside the heart of the
city, indicating that Yax Pac was willing to share even the trap-
pings of royalty to insure the loyalty of his subjects in those trou-
bled times. But conditions apparently became too hard for the
state to survive. It looks as if Yax Pac hung on as a weak king until

West face of the Labna Arch, specially lighted for this photograph, features small stone houses above two side doorways—the Maya's thatched dwellings in miniature. The portal once connected two courtyards. Though often visited in the past, Labna still awaits full scientific study.

early in the ninth century. A possible successor may be recorded on Altar L, but if indeed he was a pretender to the throne, he didn't make it, because the altar was never even finished!"

After the collapse of the royal line, those families with land-holdings in the valley—such as the family of scribes—lingered on, perhaps for as long as a century. But the glory days were over. No more temples were built, no more texts were inscribed, no more portraits were rendered. The peasants retreated to out-lying areas in the mountains, where there was still fertile soil to farm. By the end of the ninth century, Copan had become a ghost town. For generations afterward, farmers remembered and re-turned as pilgrims to leave offerings and visit the sacred land-

scape. One by one other great centers emptied as the system collapsed and trade, economy, and leadership failed; Quirigua, Palenque, Tikal, and others met the same fate as Copan.

The Yucatan Peninsula seems an unlikely area for new Maya cities to have developed in late Classic times. Its massive limestone shelf stretches flat and almost featureless. Nature's drama seems to take place above the earth in the all-encompassing sky: Sunrise, sunset, and cloud formations of a rainy-season storm have a visual impact the visitor never forgets. Thin topsoil covers the peninsula, and no streams flow there except in the south. While a few lakes dot the easternmost areas, Yucatan, for the most part, stretches hot, dry, and covered in scrub forest to

every horizon. The land's only hills form a V-shaped basin near the center of the peninsula and enclose relatively deep, rich soil. There, the Classic Maya rose to brief urban glory about A.D. 800 as Copan and other centers failed.

Within the Puuc—"range of hills" in Yucatec Maya—these later cities sit close to one another like jewels clustered in a setting. "It's the location of some of the most spectacular Maya buildings," archaeologist Jeremy Sabloff of the University of Pittsburgh told me. "I would argue, as others have, that they mark the height of pre-Columbian architectural achievement in the whole New World." The architectural style employs plates of limestone over rubble cores and facades of thousands of stones set in intricate and repetitive designs like mosaics. Many of them represent the long-nosed face of Chaac, the rain god.

Understandably, for the Puuc area has no cenotes, limestone sinkholes that served as natural wells for prehistoric peoples of northern Yucatan. People of the Puuc depended solely on water they stored during the rainy season. In a bountiful year, rain falls daily from June into November. Dry months forced the

Sunset after a storm illumines buildings at Uxmal, among the greatest glories of Puuc architecture. The huge Pyramid of the Magician and the Monjas, or "Nunnery," quadrangle lie beyond the Palace of the Governor, whose frieze typifies the intricate facades of Puuc structures. The double-headed stone jaguar at left probably served as a throne.

THRONE, C. 3 FEET LONG

157

*Ornamentation
approaches obsession on
the Palace of the Masks
at Kabah. Some 250
masks of the Maya rain
god, Chaac, blanket the
facade in rows. The roof
comb forms a stepped fret
pattern; pieces of it lie
on the ground awaiting
restoration. Maya artists
also found inspiration
in everyday life—as
reflected by the Jaina
figurine of a woman
with a bowl at left.*

Maya to use water stored in reservoirs, large drainage basins, and bell-shaped cisterns called chultunes dug into bedrock.

Comparatively few inscriptions adorn Puuc cities; no wealth of dates and dynasties aids scholars with clues to the past. Some of the inscriptions indicate that many royal leaders honored the rain god by taking the title Lord Chaac, further attesting to that deity's importance.

Lack of inscriptions is not the only reason for the dearth of information. Uxmal, the best known of the Puuc cities, has thousands of visitors a year, yet the city remains relatively untouched by scholars. Excavations have been few and little more than superficial. No one has fully mapped Uxmal or traced its boundaries. No one can even guess its ancient population.

"It amazes me," Jerry Sabloff said. "There're so few data. You take two steps away from the architecture into the bush and you're in the unknown. Puuc sites had a great florescence in A.D. 800 as centers to the south changed or were abandoned. It lasted until about 1000. Some argue that maybe people from the south moved north. We don't know. We can't even say if this florescence happened over one generation or several."

Invocations in stone, Chaac masks of Kabah echo Maya farmers' prayers for rain. By A.D. 900, most Classic Maya centers in the south lay abandoned, their end hastened perhaps by ecological problems and outside pressures. Maya cities of the Puuc endured for another hundred years, until they, too, were eclipsed.

Jerry, his colleagues, and students have worked several seasons mapping the site of Sayil. "The map is the first indication of a Puuc city's size and population," Jerry told me. "Now Gair Tourtellot, the project's co-director, and I are able to define the site's boundaries. The urban part covers more than a square mile. Within that area we found some 2,400 cultural features, from a palace to modest houses and chultunes. There's a ball court and what may have been a market. The urban area doesn't just flow into the hinterland. Stone buildings, other structures, and chultunes stop, and on at least two sides large rubble pyramids appear to serve as boundary markers. Almost everything dates roughly from the eighth century to the eleventh. There are more than 200 stone buildings at Sayil, including the huge three-story Great Palace, with some 90 rooms, built over a period of time.

"Here, in a relatively small area, we have major cities cheek by jowl. Kabah lies only four miles north of Sayil, with Labna about four miles to the east, and a large number of smaller sites in between, but we don't know their relationships. We know about the southern sites in terms of politics, economy, and development through intensive research and the information hieroglyphs are giving us. But without such knowledge about Puuc sites, most questions about their growth are currently unanswerable. We have to go past palaces and temples to the peasants. We must try to understand the total settlement picture, not just part.

"What was the political and economic organization of these centers? I think they had a central organization for water control. There must have been some overarching political authority in the area. A major system of control, with intercommunity cooperation, was successful late and only for a short period. Theirs was a very precarious situation. They couldn't have left it to chance. They had to have enough drinking water to survive."

There is one permanent water source near Sayil. Jerry described it as an underground pool deep within a cave called Gruta de Chaac—Cave of Chaac. The Maya avoided building a city anywhere near it, thus creating a kind of no-man's-land.

"Not an everyday source," said Jerry. "It must have had tremendous ritual importance and great ideological connotations— a kind of sacred landscape. No one battled to control it, and sites were located well away."

During the dry season, Maya farmers of Yucatan still gather to offer gifts and ritually beg Chaac's blessing on a parched land. As the sun makes its way through the underworld, they chant traditional prayers from dusk to dawn, just as their ancestors must have done. An intricate Puuc design on a building at Kabah serves as a riveting reminder of the ancient obsession with water and, therefore, survival. Mosaic faces of Chaac cover the entire facade of the building in rows that repeat and repeat. "Chaac, Chaac, Chaac," they say, and again, "Chaac," as if in a litany in praise of water, in an unending prayer for rain. ∎

160

Trade and EMPIRE

"The Mesoamerican idea of a city was imbedded in . . . the workings of nature. . . ."

FOLLOWING PAGES: Signal
fires guide cargo-laden
canoes to the beach below
the Castillo—and alert
residents to the arrival of
travelers. By A.D. 900,
large oceangoing vessels
like these transported
trade goods over great
distances. Tulum,
commanding a seaside
cliff, became a port of call
on the Yucatan coast in
late Postclassic times.

T wo weeks out of Cuba and a new age away from
Spain, four ships bearing some 200 men sailed boldly
into the unknown. It was April of 1518 when explorer
Juan de Grijalva, pursuing reports of new lands rich
with gold, led his small fleet past Cape Catoche, the northeastern
tip of Yucatan. The peninsula had been discovered by earlier adventurers, but none had explored its eastern coast. Grijalva and
his men continued southward, venturing into uncharted waters
along mysterious shores.

The expedition reached the island of Cozumel, where, according to one member, there were three large towns. Grijalva
stood on a Maya temple containing idols and human bones to
claim possession of the island for his king. The Spaniards found
the settlements there far more impressive than the small Caribbean island villages they had seen. Intrigued, they pressed southward. "We followed the shore day and night," Grijalva's
chaplain, Juan Díaz, recorded, "and the next day toward sunset
we perceived a city or town so large, that Seville would not have
seemed more considerable nor better; one saw there a very large
tower; on the shore was a great throng of Indians, who bore two
standards which they raised and lowered to signal us to ap-
proach them; the commander did not wish it."

Though Díaz exaggerated its size, scholars believe the city
was probably Tulum, a Postclassic Maya center rising dramatically on a limestone promontory. The large tower likely was the
highest part of the Castillo, a cliffside temple that dominates the
site. Below and to one side a breach in the steep cliffs shelters a
narrow sandy beach—then a landing area for native trading canoes. The smooth stretch also would have been easily defended
by a few warriors deployed above it. Grijalva was probably pru-
dent to ignore the signals from shore and continue his journey.

While cliffs edged the town to seaward, massive walls completed the other three sides of Tulum's rectangular plan. They
date from the city's founding in about A.D. 1200, and in places
they were 10 to 15 feet high and 20 feet thick. Five gates in the
walls gave access to the town, and one still does, leading visitors
into the 16-acre enclosure. I have always found it a delightful sur-
prise to enter the narrow stone passageway and emerge as if by
magic within an ancient city.

Tulum was one of the few Postclassic centers the Spaniards
did not destroy and rebuild, or that did not topple of its own ac-
cord. Late Maya settlements were, for the most part, ineptly constructed, and Tulum was no exception. In fact, the whole city sits
askew. Buildings are squat, almost miniature; doorways seem
too small for easy entrance. Temples appear to lean, walls to bow
outward. Crooked columns wobble upward in miraculous feats
of survival. Relatively shoddy stonework was once concealed by
thick stucco, much as uneven cake layers are hidden by generous
applications of icing. Still, the ruins attest to deceptively strong,

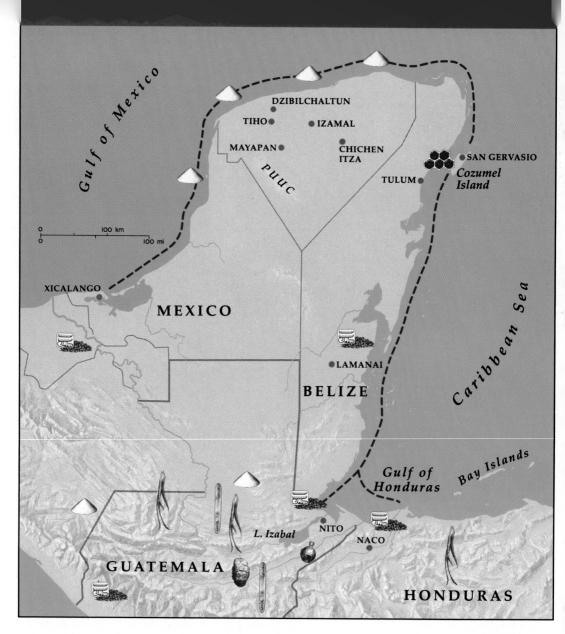

The Postclassic period, from around A.D. 900 to 1500, saw
the rise of a mercantile class in Mesoamerica. With the
collapse of Teotihuacan and the decline of Classic Maya
city-states, a seafaring people known as the Putun assumed
the role of procuring and exporting raw materials and other
goods. Their main sea route, shown on the map, linked the
Gulf coast of Yucatan, close to overland trade routes from
the highlands, with ports on the other side of the peninsula.
Cozumel Island served as a way station and storage depot.
The Putun handled a wide variety of goods, including
copper, jade, and quetzal plumes for ornaments and
ceremonial dress; honey and salt; obsidian for blades; cacao
beans, used as currency as well as for chocolate drinks; and
cotton, ceramics, shells, stingray spines, and slaves.

MAP ART BY TIBOR G. TOTH

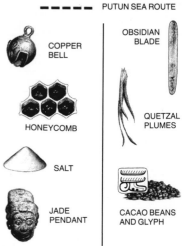

- - - - - PUTUN SEA ROUTE

COPPER
BELL

HONEYCOMB

SALT

JADE
PENDANT

OBSIDIAN
BLADE

QUETZAL
PLUMES

CACAO BEANS
AND GLYPH

if unattractive, construction, and the remaining stucco is of high quality. It often bears sections of murals expertly executed on the interiors and exteriors of temples.

The murals show deities and rituals painted in bright colors with dark outlines and constrained within rigid borders. Such art holds clues to Postclassic urban Yucatan, and suggests that Maya culture had become a blend. Influences from highland Mexico had left their impact, for the murals reflect the Mixtec manuscript art style of Oaxaca. But the gods are chiefly Maya; some murals show what may be Chaac, the rain god. Sculptures of descending winged gods first seen in Puuc architecture of the Classic period reappeared centuries later on buildings at Tulum.

A study of the site in the 1950s by archaeologist William T. Sanders of Pennsylvania State University revealed a master plan. Most structures were oriented to one axis; about 24 buildings in two rows fronted a main street, and nearly all were residential. Between 30 and 40 more houses lay in a terraced area. Religious structures were grouped together in a ceremonial center.

Dr. Sanders estimates that when its population peaked in the first half of the 15th century, Tulum had 500 to 600 permanent residents, and about 350 to 400 of them lived in working-class or military-class housing. The elaborate stone palaces of more elite residents indicated a rising political caste. The population, Dr. Sanders suggests, was strictly ordered in a confined space with regularly placed "streets." He also notes that the total population remained small, probably because of the difficulty of producing and transporting food in that part of the Yucatan Peninsula.

In both plan and style, Tulum and other Yucatecan cities of the period differed markedly from Classic Maya centers. Gone were masterfully wrought monuments to god-kings and exquisite multiroomed palaces. Soaring temple-pyramids and religious centers built as cosmic metaphors had become less vital as concepts. Architecture was simply no longer as important as it had been in earlier times. Did this reflect a less important role for religion in Postclassic Maya society?

"The religious sphere shifted," archaeologist Jeremy Sabloff told me. "Some scholars believe religion was just as important as before, but had a different emphasis. It was not controlled in the same way. The Postclassic Maya didn't have central labor investments such as huge temples. Instead, they had family oratories and incense burners." What had brought about this change?

"Evidence points to environmental degradation, if not major catastrophes, in the southern lowlands at the end of the Classic period," Jerry said. "The cities that continued after A.D. 800 tended to be places on the coast or with river access to the sea along trade routes, or places that could cultivate cacao or cotton or produce salt for trade. Cities that survived or flourished were the ones that had resources or still-fertile lands. In the Postclassic the whole economy shifted. This led to significant cultural changes."

Conferring on matters of state, the sumptuously attired rulers of Cozumel, Izamal, and Mayapan stroll through an open colonnade near the main temple complex at Mayapan. Headdresses, loincloths, and other features of their elegant garb are based on murals, bas-reliefs, codices, and incense burners like the one opposite, a clay effigy of the long-nosed rain god, Chaac. Smoke from burning copal resin wafts from the Chaac censer on the altar.

According to scholars, the Postclassic period began around A.D. 900 with the final abandonment of the Classic Maya cities in the lowlands, some 200 years after the collapse of Teotihuacan in the highlands. Then pre-Columbian Mesoamerica entered its last great era, which was distinguished by an increased emphasis on militarism and trade.

Written annals compiled after the conquest also set the Postclassic apart from previous periods. Surviving Classic Maya glyphs record cycles of time and hierarchies of gods, as well as genealogies and historic and religious events, but these mainly concerned the elite. Spanish accounts, together with native chronicles, record more general events dating back more than 500 years—to the beginning of the Postclassic and before. Myth, however, clouds many native histories, sometimes making it impossible to determine which portions have a firm basis in fact.

According to Aztec history, the Toltecs attained power in the highlands in the tenth century, after the fall of Teotihuacan. Sixteenth-century Aztec accounts credited them with amazing accomplishments: "The Toltecs were wise. Their works were all good, all perfect, all wonderful, all marvelous; their houses

beautiful, tiled in mosaics, smoothed, stuccoed. . . ." The name of their legendary capital, Tollan, or Tula—literally, "place of reeds"—came to mean "city." Most scholars locate the capital in the present-day ruins of Tula in the Mexican state of Hidalgo.

Also according to the Aztecs, Quetzalcoatl—Feathered Serpent—ruled Tula as a benevolent priest-king and worshiper of the god of the same name. In A.D. 987, followers of Tezcatlipoca, god of warriors, giver and taker of life, drove the priest-king and his disciples out of Tula. One myth says Quetzalcoatl set himself on fire and his heart rose into the heavens to become Morning Star; another says he fled to the Gulf coast and traveled eastward on a raft of serpents, vowing to return and reclaim his domain.

Maya chronicles also tell of a mighty warrior, a conqueror who arrived in Yucatan by sea from the west—also in A.D. 987. In

Maya his name was Kukulcan—Feathered Serpent—and they said he conquered the peninsula and set up his capital at a place later called Chichen Itza. How much truth can be gleaned from these intriguing coincidences? For decades scholars have seen a connection between Tula and Chichen; in art, architecture, and other ways they are strikingly similar, yet the Toltec question remains one of the most fascinating mysteries of ancient Mesoamerica—and a subject of considerable dispute. Most scholars believe the Toltecs swept out of the highlands and gained an empire, but some have questioned the very existence of the Toltecs as a cultural group. Some also question the importance of Tula in Hidalgo. After all, Chichen Itza is larger and more skillfully built. To confuse the issue further, traditional Puuc and Toltec architecture sit cheek by jowl at Chichen and seem contemporary.

Accompanying her husband, Rik, on assignment, Bronwyn Cooke scales the Temple of Kukulcan at Mayapan. The walled city dominated northern Yucatan from about 1250 to 1450. Nature reclaimed the abandoned site, still largely unexcavated. Fig tree roots (opposite) slowly reduce a vault to rubble.

Modern Mexico City
surrounds the remains of
the Great Temple, heart
of the Aztec capital of
Tenochtitlan. The 1978
discovery of a huge stone
disk at the pyramid's
base led to intensive
excavation of the site.
Cracked by weight and
stress, the carved
monolith depicts the
goddess Coyolxauhqui,
slain and dismembered
by her brother, the war
god Huitzilopochtli, the
Aztecs' tribal deity.

DAVID HISER

Now, new discoveries are dispelling the mythical mist that enshrouds the Toltecs. Archaeologist Charles E. Lincoln has worked at Chichen, and he told me of his findings. "In iconography, ethnohistory, and archaeology, evidence indicates a dual monarchy emerged at Chichen Itza sometime after A.D. 800," he said. "It happened in response to Maya social disintegration. I see at Chichen an innovative reformation of Maya society. The city did not witness an invasion from outside the realm, but an in-place evolution."

By the end of the 12th century Tula had collapsed, and Toltec power ended in Yucatan shortly thereafter. Whoever the Toltecs had been, they passed through the centuries from glorious memory into magical myth.

Trade intensified in Postclassic times as a people called the Putun plied Mexico's Gulf and Caribbean coasts in large canoes and brought Yucatan into their orbit. These foreigners were probably Chontal Maya from Tabasco and southern Campeche who had come under highland Mexican influence and become far-ranging merchants and mercenaries. Perhaps the Putun, and not the Toltecs themselves, were responsible for spreading Toltec influences. Putun trade networks stretched from Mexico through Central America.

Like the Putun traders, a group called the Itza came as intruders into Yucatan. They may have come in with the Putun, or the two may in fact have been the same people. They arrived sometime after 1200. Yucatecan chronicles spoke of the Itza's wandering migration out of Tabasco and referred to them as "those who speak our language brokenly." The Maya of Yucatan, ever-conscious of family name, lineage, and inherited status, scorned them as people "without fathers and mothers."

Following a leader who, perhaps by shrewd design, claimed the title Kukulkan as his Toltec predecessor had done, the Itza, according to tradition, settled in an abandoned city by 1224 and gave it the name Chichen Itza. By 1283, Chichen fell in a conflict among Itza factions, and the victors made the recently founded city of Mayapan their capital.

I visited Mayapan on a hot, humid day of alternating sunshine and storm. The ruins lie in an area of uneven, stony terrain unsuitable for agriculture. I later asked Jeremy Sabloff why the Itza chose such an unpromising spot. "It may be that it was still a central location after Chichen fell," he said. "It may have been the number of cenotes—good permanent water sources. It may have had something to do with Maya power bases and ruling families. Clearly it was not built for agricultural potential." Mayapan, Jerry pointed out, fulfilled a power potential and fulfilled it well. Chronicles say that Yucatan had been previously divided into independent provinces. Now the Itza summoned provincial

rulers and their families and retainers to Mayapan and held them for ransom—namely, tribute from the lands they controlled. Mayapan had no need for agricultural fields, since food and other goods poured into the city from pressured provinces.

The royal house of Cocom assumed power in Mayapan. "All the lords took care to respect, visit, and entertain Cocom, accompanying him, feasting him, and coming to him with difficult business. . . . and spent much time in the amusements to which they are accustomed, such as dancing, banquets, and hunting," wrote Bishop Diego de Landa, a Spanish chronicler of Yucatan. Provincial majordomos told each town "what was required in the lord's house by way of fowl, maize, honey, salt, fish, game, clothing, and other items."

Had I not been forewarned, I would never have guessed that the ruins surrounding me were those of an important capital. The Temple of Kukulcan, a shabby and shrunken copy of Chichen's main temple-pyramid, rises near the center of the site. It, too, honored the Feathered Serpent god, but in a version made of poorly cut stone covered with stucco. Nearby lie the remains of a colonnaded structure decorated with masks of the rain god Chaac. Stone serpent heads adorn a restored temple on a small pyramid. But only that central area has been cleared; a trail leads through part of the site where most of Mayapan's buildings long ago slumped into pathetic piles of rubble now obscured by dense forest. I sought shelter from mosquito hordes among the few partially standing buildings, and on a smooth stone I spread a map made by archaeologists in the 1950s. Only then did I realize the scope of the ancient city.

A stone wall 19 feet thick in places and penetrated by 12 gates had enclosed an urban complex of about one and a half square miles shaped like a gigantic teardrop. Some 4,000 structures crowded the area within the wall, but only about 140 could be called ceremonial buildings, and most of those lay near the center, ranged around the Temple of Kukulcan. The rest were houses or parts of residential compounds.

Terrain had determined the city's layout, with householders preferring hillocks. A causeway led to a "palace" perhaps grand enough for a Cocom, but most residents had modest two-room dwellings. Low walls enclosed house groups probably occupied by related families.

"The city 'pattern' is completely haphazard: there are no streets, no arrangement to be discerned at all, and it seems as if the basically dispersed Maya had been forced by the Itza to live jam-packed together within the walls in a kind of urban anarchy," commented archaeologist Michael D. Coe. "No city like it had ever been seen before in the Maya area."

Perhaps 11,000 to 12,000 people lived in Mayapan. Miserable congestion, oppressive heat, and sanitation problems must have plagued the crowded capital.

Chronicles say foreigners known as the Xiu, who had been living near the ruins of Uxmal, overthrew the Cocom dynasty around 1446. Yucatan split into 16 small independent states, much like those of Classic Maya times, and a Maya seer wrote in lyric verse a prophecy of foreigners to come: "Receive your guests, the bearded men, the men who come from the east. . . . The change will be manifest to all."

Those Spaniards who had sailed past Tulum explored as far as Ascension Bay, retraced their peninsular route, and visited Maya settlements along the Gulf coast. There they encountered hostility, but also found what they had been seeking—gold, if only a few trinkets. Juan de Grijalva sent news of this back to Cuba, whereupon leaders of New Spain, in hope of vast treasure, mounted another expedition—a fateful one. When ships again sailed from Cuba to the mainland in February 1519, their charismatic captain, Hernán Cortés, unknowingly had begun a journey toward Mesoamerica's greatest Postclassic city, Tenochtitlan, and into the heart of the Aztec empire.

Tasseled headdress and shawl may identify this polished stone figure as Chalchiuhtlicue, Aztec goddess of water. Carvings of the deity in the style of Tenochtitlan indicate her significance for that island city. Associating stone with permanence and the glories of past civilizations, the Aztecs frequently used it for large and small sculptures alike.

C. 30 INCHES HIGH

Who were the Aztecs? They came from a place of myth and dreams, an island they called Aztlan, from which they began their centuries-long tribal wanderings. The Aztecs, or Mexica, liked to stress their hardscrabble heritage—one of poor hunters often reduced to eating snakes and vermin, unfortunates who had pulled themselves up by their own sandal straps from poverty to power.

"Their ancient accounts of wandering riffraff may have been partly true," archaeologist Susan Evans told me. "But they probably came from a fairly sophisticated area of northwestern Mexico and shared a general culture with other speakers of the Nahuatl language living in the Basin of Mexico. They most likely took up nomadism because of climatic changes around A.D. 1000. They had to abandon their homeland, move on, and reestablish themselves as a settled people."

By their own accounts, the Aztecs wandered toward small city-states in the Valley of Mexico. For generations they lived as a bellicose group despised by all whom they encountered. For a time they stayed in the Toltec city of Tula. As they went along, beset by tribulations, they cried out for divine mercy and in answer heard revelations of dreams from their priests. The gods spoke only through those sacred leaders, and the people listened and obeyed. "They believed that the earth had been promised to them by their gods," wrote a 16th-century Spanish friar and historian, Fray Diego Durán.

Huitzilopochtli, the Aztecs' tribal god, their bloodthirsty god of war, was probably a deified early leader. Demanding and unforgiving, he fed upon human hearts. Durán wrote that Huitzilopochtli promised to reward the suffering of his people: "He

177

will make them lords of gold and silver. . . . the Aztecs will build houses and temples of jade and rubies in his name. . . ."

The Aztecs entered the Valley of Mexico by the mid-13th century. They first settled at Chapultepec, but were driven out by local people. They became serfs and then warriors of the cultivated people of Culhuacan south of Lake Texcoco. They offended their overlords with their cruelty, and when they sacrificed a Culhuacan princess given as bride to their chief, they were expelled. In 1325 the wanderers established themselves on an island in the lake and, as Huitzilopochtli had commanded, began to build a city on the spot where an eagle perched on a cactus. They called their city Tenochtitlan. Later, dissident factions founded another city, Tlatelolco, on a nearby island. Both cities flourished, with Tenochtitlan becoming dominant.

The Aztecs were the fiercest warriors in central Mexico, and they had entered the basin in the power vacuum left by Tula's fall. They served as mercenaries of neighboring Tepanec kings, who ruled from their capital of Azcapotzalco on the northwestern shore of the lake. Under Tepanec tutelage, opportunistic Aztecs mastered statecraft and empire building—and in 1428 overthrew Azcapotzalco and became independent.

Intricate picture writing fills a page of the Codex Borgia, a book of sacred lore produced in Mexico before 1519. Skilled scribes painted such documents on long sheets of deerskin or bark paper, folded like screens. Metalwork set the Postclassic apart from earlier periods, but few gold artifacts escaped Spanish looting. A miniature shield and a pendant, both with bells, and a bracelet (opposite) were recovered from the Gulf of Mexico in 1976.

Through shrewd political marriages, Aztecs now had divine kings of ancient Toltec lineage instead of tribal chiefs; now alliances with other cities strengthened them; now rulers of other states bowed to them; now they had an expanding empire of their own. By the time Cortés arrived, Tenochtitlan was the most magnificent city in Mesoamerica, and a dream had been fulfilled. An exultant Aztec poet sang: "Extended lies the city, lies Mexico, spreading circles of emerald light, radiating splendor like a quetzal plume. Beside her the boats of the war chiefs come and go. A flower-mist spreads out above the people." And another poet arrogantly asked: "Who could conquer Tenochtitlan? Who could shake the foundation of heaven?"

In 1502 the Aztecs installed their ninth king and their last independent ruler, known today as Moctezuma II. By the time Cortés drew near, the king seemed more preoccupied with portents than with military prowess. For a decade, evil omens had plagued the credulous emperor. In 1518 Grijalva's ships exploring near modern Veracruz caused dreadful foreboding: News reached Moctezuma that great towers or small mountains had been sighted floating on the sea.

Through myth the Aztecs recalled that the exiled priest-king, Quetzalcoatl, had vowed to return and reclaim his domain. When the small Spanish army, numbering about 400 men, together with Indian allies, came within sight of the city, Moctezuma vacillated, fearing Cortés to be the Toltec deity returning as promised. He allowed the Spanish conquerer into Tenochtitlan, thus sealing the fate of his empire.

The Spaniards were awed by what they saw—"a very large city, built in the water like Venice," one reported. Wide causeways led from the mainland to the twin island cities. Masonry aqueducts carried massive flows of spring water; a huge dike built by the king of allied Texcoco separated the lake's salty eastern sector from the area of fresh water surrounding the cities and the fertile chinampas to the south. What was once marshland had become a metropolis covering about 5 square miles, with a population perhaps as large as 200,000 living in some 60,000 houses. No wonder the Spaniards were overwhelmed. Toledo around that time had only 18,000 inhabitants, and Seville, the city Spaniards had compared to Tulum, some 45,000.

Wide avenues divided Tenochtitlan into four quadrants. Intersecting canals and streets subdivided the city. Many of these "city blocks" were built-up chinampas with flower and vegetable gardens. Scholars see in this geometric layout an echo of the urban plan of nearby Teotihuacan; certainly Aztecs were aware of that ancient city. Scholars also believe the layout of Tenochtitlan reflects a social and political organization known to have been highly stratified and rigidly controlled.

Three main groups composed Aztec society. At the top of the social pyramid, noblemen, or *pipiltin,* held offices in the imperial administration. The *macehualtin*—commoners—included most of the population, and they lived in districts comparable to wards or barrios, which were divided into groups of houses or households for administrative purposes. Bondsmen tilled the lands of the pipiltin. Captive slaves and those who sold themselves into slavery had little status in Aztec society.

The Aztecs' power depended on the activities of two typically Postclassic groups: long-distance traders and warriors. The former obtained exotic materials such as quetzal plumes, jade, and jaguar skins for royalty and also served as far-ranging spies. They amassed wealth of their own, but carefully concealed their private stores so as not to arouse jealousy. They dressed modestly and entered the city with their goods at night. Partly to maintain their status, these rich merchants entertained each other and the nobility at lavish feasts, and provided slaves for sacrifice. But the machinery of state was geared to war, and merchants and even priests sometimes served as soldiers.

"Until Moctezuma felt the noble class was big enough and brought the practice to a stop, social mobility was available to any warrior who could fight his way up and take a certain number of captives," Susan Evans said. "Among the prizes were land and the fruits of that land. This kind of expansion was an important way to win a place in society. Heroes could become nobles."

At Huitzilopochtli's command, Aztec warriors expanded the empire through aggression. They also fought in prearranged "Flowery Wars," battles waged solely to capture sacrificial victims; flowers were a metaphor for human blood. Warriors knew no greater glory than battle. In song they proclaimed: "There is nothing like death in war, nothing like the flowery death. . . ."

This war-loving realm embraced lands from the Gulf coast to the Pacific in present-day Mexico and extended southward in some areas to the Guatemala border. The empire controlled some five to six million people. On fixed dates, tribute ranging from grain to gold poured into Tenochtitlan. "They forced people into a complex economic relationship because of the needs of empire—and they ruled by fear," Susan Evans said. Like the lords of Mayapan, Aztecs demanded rulers of conquered peoples as hostages. "Vanquished leaders had to spend part of the year in the capital and send heirs apparent there to be educated," she said. "This created an elite solidarity all over Mesoamerica— royal children knew other royal children. It also guaranteed that no one would renege on tribute."

Hostages lived in luxury in the center of the city. There the Serpent Wall enclosed the most sacred temples. Just outside the ceremonial enclosure were the finest palaces, which served as administrative offices as well. There Cortés and part of his entourage resided as Moctezuma's guests.

FOLLOWING PAGES: *In early morning mist, verdant chinampas near Mixquic, Mexico, recall those of Tenochtitlan. The Aztecs built such artificial islands by alternating layers of mud and decaying vegetation over shallow lake bottoms or in marshes. They tended the fertile platforms in flat-bottomed canoes, growing corn, squash, beans, and other vegetables, and flowers. Farmers of Mixquic follow a similar practice today.*

181

Twin temples—one blue, one red—stood atop a towering pyramid in the center of the ceremonial enclosure. These metaphors for sacred mountains expressed a duality: The blue temple honored Tlaloc, the central Mexican god of rain; the red one glorified the god Huitzilopochtli. They faced westward, aligned with the movements of the heavens. During the rainy season, the sun rose from behind the Temple of Tlaloc, and in the dry months it rose behind the Temple of Huitzilopochtli, notes art historian Mary Ellen Miller of Yale University. But on the mornings of the two annual equinoxes, the sun rose between these two temples and faced the Temple of Quetzalcoatl. The blue shrine represented water, and the red shrine, the sun. Together, they represented unity, completion, life, and seasonal renewal. Together, they are called the Great Temple.

Archaeologist Eduardo Matos Moctezuma, now director of Mexico's Museo del Templo Mayor, and his associates excavated this sacred precinct from 1978 to 1982. Their labors revealed several reconstructions of the temples over a period of nearly 200 years and a magnificent array of artifacts associated with them. I visited the excavation site and saw newly discovered Aztec heirlooms—an Olmec jade mask and several greenstone masks from Teotihuacan. A cache near the shrine of Tlaloc included Aztec vessels depicting the god, along with bones of sacrificed children. (Their tears at death, it was said, moved the god to bestow rain, and the more they wept, the more rain he would send.)

A large stone disk depicting the goddess Coyolxauhqui lay at the base of the stairway leading to the Temple of Huitzilopochtli. To the Aztecs he was the sun, and she was his sister, the moon. Huitzilopochtli defeated her and their brothers, the stars, in battle and hurled her body from the heights. Scholars see in this symbols of the Aztec concept of a constant cosmic war between day and night and the repeated triumph of the sun—and thus of the Aztecs. The goddess's dismembered body, at least one scholar suggests, may express phases of the moon.

Professor Matos has excavated another astounding discovery. "When we moved the Coyolxauhqui stone to the new Museo del Templo Mayor at the site, we exposed an earlier version beneath it," he told me. "The older one is different in style but not in concept." He sketched it for me. It, too, is a disk showing the goddess's dismembered body, but the limbs are very thin and the figure has no head. "The location of the goddess corresponds to the myth. She is to be found on the base platform, on the terrestrial level, where she has been thrown down by her victorious brother." The figure occupies only the upper part of the disk. Professor Matos sketched in the rest. "Here, a shield and arrows represent Tenochtitlan, and here, a design of intertwined serpents is a symbol for the earth."

The Aztecs also saw the earth as a landmass surrounded by water, described as a ring of turquoises. On a horizontal plane

Reconstructed Aztec sanctuary glows at dusk in Santa Cecilia Acatitlan. At such temples, fires burned in large braziers, and as crowds below watched, priests sacrificed human victims to propitiate the gods. Small, elevated shrines stood at the centers of thousands of Aztec villages; the Spaniards destroyed virtually all of them.

DAVID HISER/ASPEN

185

the universe was divided in 4 directions; vertically, earth lay in the center between the 13 heavens and the 9 levels of the underworld. "I believe the principal center, or navel, where the horizontal and vertical planes intersected was the Great Temple," said Professor Matos. "It represented the entire cosmos, where all sacred power was concentrated." Sacrificial victims by the thousand died there to propitiate demanding gods, and there, after coronation, Aztec emperors let their own blood to affirm the divine destiny of rulership.

Symbolism of architecture and landscape has long been an interest of art historian Richard F. Townsend of the Art Institute of Chicago. Sounds of a modern city drifted into his office as we discussed the relationship between nature and urbanism. "Mesoamerican attitudes differed completely from those of Western peoples," he said. "To us a city is separate from nature. It is a contained world, an internal culture. They linked sacred caves and mountains to rulership and divine support. To them, temple architecture symbolized components of a sacred landscape. The main pyramid of Tenochtitlan is an urban expression of those ideas.

"This is a basic North American Indian attitude first manifested visually on a large scale by the Olmecs. The Mesoamerican idea of a city was imbedded in and surrounded by the workings of nature—not a denial of nature, but rather a communion with it. They didn't think of cities as enclosed spaces; however large cities became, people were deeply conscious of what was happening in the environment. Natural features gave them a sense of place, and major buildings were oriented to take into account the physical environment. The city reached out and incorporated the meaning in the landscape. Mountains and caves, the rainy season and storms, not just the sun and the moon, were all key elements. The Mesoamerican social order was rooted in nature, and its activities unfolded in harmony with the cosmos."

In this cosmic calendar Aztecs saw Quetzalcoatl's prophecy fulfilled, for Cortés had arrived during the cyclical time the god had foretold—and in the end had attacked. With cataclysmic battles and fires raging in Tenochtitlan, the cycle of Aztec supremacy was completed. By mid-August 1521, the last Aztec king, Cuauhtemoc, had surrendered. Blood, for which flowers were a metaphor, stained the beautiful houses and flowed in the canals.

For the Aztecs, flowers were associated with poetry, and poetic skill was as precious to kings as warfare. At Tenochtitlan's zenith, a poet had asked: "Will I have to go like the flowers that perish? Will nothing remain of my name? Nothing of my fame here on earth?" A poet of the Otomi, a subject people, wrote as if in reply: "The river passes, passes, never stops. The wind passes, passes, never stops. Life passes, never returns." ∎

EPILOGUE

In the darkest hours before dawn, when birds have not yet begun to sing, while insects of the night still hum and unseen creatures steal through the forest, men of the modern village of Coba in northern Yucatan honor an ancient stone monument with a figure carved on it. The stone stands before a lofty pyramid known as the Iglesia, or Church. As they set out to hunt deer, the men reverently offer gifts of food and light beeswax candles to the carving, and beseech its aid. Local Maya see in the eroded figure an ancestral deity, and they call it a mother goddess. Archaeologists see in it the portrait of a king who ruled the Classic Maya city of Coba, and they call it Stela 11.

Archaeologists say the Maya abandoned Coba shortly after the Spanish conquest, dispersing to farms and settlements. Villagers say the ancients went to the coast and put out to sea, but God made their vessels sink and they drowned. For centuries jaguars, monkeys, and other tropical animals prowled deserted palaces and temples as the forest gradually reclaimed the site. Then, in the 1940s, Maya families from nearby settlements created a new village in the heart of the old city.

Adventurers and archaeologists visited the ruins briefly from time to time and marveled at what they saw, but for the most part ancient Coba remained one of countless sites wrapped in mystery. Then, in the 1970s, research teams from Mexico and the United States began investigations. William Folan, now of the Universidad del Sudeste in Campeche, Mexico, and my husband, National Geographic staff archaeologist George Stuart, headed the American team. My family and I lived in the ruins for a total of seven months, and others spent longer periods there. Although little of the site has been excavated, much of it has now been mapped, and the international effort revealed amazing facts that distinguish Coba from other Maya cities.

Remains of modest dwellings extend for miles beneath the forest canopy, but the main ruins center on two lakes, rare features in a region of scarce surface water. Evidence shows

Discolored fragment of a stela, the monument of a Maya king, today holds sacred meaning for villagers of Coba in northern Yucatan. To invoke divine aid in hunting, they place gifts of food and candles at the stone, below the pyramid known as the Iglesia.

that people lived there in Preclassic times, but has not yet disclosed the scope of their settlement. It was in the Classic period that Coba reached the peak of its glory, booming into one of the largest of all Maya cities. An estimated 50,000 people lived in the metropolis, which spread over some 25 square miles.

Four major concentrations of buildings constituted "downtown"; one is called the Coba group. "It includes what is surely one of the most complicated aggregates of ancient architecture to be found at any ancient Maya city," George says. Platforms, patios, plazas, stairs, and quadrangles of vaulted buildings sit in complex juxtaposition. Though it focuses on the Iglesia pyramid, the group appears to have been largely residential. One sunken private patio opened only onto a lake. We have stood there hip-deep in undergrowth among the crumbling palatial buildings that surround it as cool breezes set Spanish moss swaying on massive trees. We have watched glittering flocks of small parrots fly overhead and a bright toucan glide past. There one feels completely isolated from the rest of the city and needs little imagination to re-create Classic royal elegance.

The Nohoch Mul, less than a mile away, is a more monumental complex, with an aura of concentrated religious ritual. The group takes its name from the Nohoch Mul—Big Mound—a pyramid rising more than 82 feet above a plaza. Beside it, engulfed in forest, bulks a massive platform measuring about 400 feet to a side and rising more than 65 feet in zones roughly equivalent to four stories; vaulted rooms, uncounted and unexplored, honeycomb the structure. "It is one of the most massive constructions in the entire Maya area," George says. "Standing on top is like being on a plateau."

Four great artificial roadways terminate near the Nohoch Mul. In Yucatec Maya these are called *sacbeob*—white roads. Other Maya cities had them, but Coba had more—a vast network of 43 raised roads totaling almost 96 miles and containing more than 1.5 million cubic yards of stone. What purpose did the sacbeob serve? Scholars have speculated that they were used for ceremonial processions or were meant as statements of aggression. They may have been symbols of elite marriage alliances or perhaps, in part, work projects to keep restless masses occupied.

Carved stelae reflect Coba's dominance in the northern plains, for the city was the capital of a powerful province. Often these monuments show kings resplendent in quetzal plumes standing on cowering prisoners. Most record events from A.D. 613 to 672, when Coba was at its height. The most recent portrays a ruler in A.D. 780, elegant in jade jewelry and jaguar skins.

The U.S. and Mexican investigating teams found that, like many other Classic cities, Coba had failed, possibly affected by climatic changes. "I think it lay abandoned for several centuries," George says. "Then about 1100 or 1200 it was reoccupied." During this Postclassic revival, builders erected squat, rather shoddy temples similar to those at Tulum and decorated them with murals of ritual dates and gods. They built pole-and-thatch houses on the great platform beside the Nohoch Mul and constructed new temples on old pyramids. By then the stelae had toppled; the Postclassic Maya saw them as useful building stones, antique curiosities, or perhaps seeds of myth.

Today, people of recent settlements near Coba regard the ancient city as a fearsome mystery. Some warned archaeologist Karl Taube of Yale University away from the ruins.

"They fear Coba," Karl said. "They told me it is dangerous at night, for in the darkness great winged serpents rise from the lakes and fly among the ruins. These are nasty, demonic creatures, especially dangerous on certain dates. One is the 15th of September, when the President of Mexico gives the Grita de Dolores—the traditional cry for revolution—right after midnight. On that date they dare not go near Coba."

Mosaic jade mask immortalizes a young adult ruler of Calakmul, a regional capital of the Maya in the present-day Mexican state of Campeche. Among the most striking pieces of Mesoamerican art yet found in this century, the portrait emerged from a royal tomb discovered by chance in 1984.

For more than five years William Folan and his associates have worked at Calakmul, a Maya site deep in eastern Campeche. From the time of the Spanish conquest Calakmul lay in isolation; few visitors made their way to it. "We discovered a Preclassic city that probably equaled El Mirador in size," Will told me. "We can stand on either of the two main structures and see El Mirador, 23 miles away. The relationship is one of the most incredible things I've ever seen. One building complex is the same size and shape as the Tigre group there. I believe they may have been twin cities, regional capitals of primitive states and probably related to a common ancestor symbolized by these twin complexes.

"Calakmul grew during the Classic period. It really took off and eventually covered at least 27 square miles. I'd say it equaled Tikal and Coba in size and population—all three were major regional capitals. The city followed a concentric plan, with most of the major architecture in the middle. There are 564 vaulted buildings in the $11\frac{1}{2}$ square miles we have mapped so far, some in quadrangular groups as large as those at Uxmal."

Through inscriptions on some of the city's 105 stelae, names of kings and their wives came to light. While digging for pottery samples, Will found a Classic royal tomb containing a lifelike jade portrait mask—one of the most impressive Mesoamerican art discoveries of the century. To stand in the Museo Regional de Campeche and look at it is like meeting a great leader of a thousand years ago face-to-face. Those Classic Maya rulers and most of their subjects abandoned Calakmul in the ninth century.

"There was a Postclassic occupation with the worst architecture I have ever seen anywhere," said Will. "It's ten times worse than Mayapan and looks like 12-year-olds built it, though I think Calakmul was the capital of a Postclassic province mentioned in the chronicles. So the site contains information we need to better understand Maya urbanism and state formation through time.

"The forest cover has helped protect Calakmul. We're not dealing with an area that has been plowed over like the Copan Valley and other sites. Also, the nearest settlement is 22 miles away, and there's no road. It's in the middle of nowhere."

Archaeologists know that forests in the middle of nowhere still conceal lost cities; as recently as 1987 there were reports of a Classic Maya site with temples still intact near the border between Mexico and Guatemala. And even many known ruins have never been mapped or excavated; "another Monte Alban" lies in the mountains south of that Oaxaca city.

Studies in the past two decades have corrected misconceptions about ancient urban North America. Until the 1960s archaeologists rarely used the term "city" when describing places like Moundville or Coba. They saw them as mystical ceremonial centers occupied only by priests and their retainers except when local villagers gathered there on ritual occasions. Now we see these places as the burgeoning towns and cities they were. Now we know the names of Maya kings who conquered, or submitted to defeat. Names of honored Maya artists have been read on pottery and stelae. No longer do we see the Maya as stargazers or the Aztecs as barbarians. In recent decades scholars have humanized ancient city builders and extended North America's written history centuries back in time.

Yet large mysteries remain unsolved. We don't know the role agriculture played in urban development in the Southeast. We don't know the extent of Mesoamerican influence in the Southwest. After years of study, Teotihuacan's kings remain anonymous; we have yet to learn how the metropolis was administered or who owned the farmland that fed this ancient North American city; we don't even know what language the people spoke. As has been said of another culture, "We know how the Hopewell died, but not how they lived."

Scholars can devote lifetimes to probing one ancient mystery perhaps enveloped in lore. "If and when in the future the mystery is solved, it will not tie things together neatly but will beget a new and even more interesting puzzle," says Mexican archaeologist Jaime Litvak King. "That is the real charm of archaeology: not what old mysteries it solves, but what new ones it poses."

Along with new mysteries, new lore will surely arise. As scholars bend to their task, others also seek explanations. They call upon traditions and myths thousands of years old. Living in the shadows of ancient cities, they listen to the rhythms of the universe and interpret their own heritage as a cycle not yet complete while they bow before dawn to an ancient goddess or tremble in the night at the rustle of serpent wings. ■

ACKNOWLEDGMENTS

The Special Publications Division is particularly grateful to Bennie C. Keel, Consulting Archaeologist for the National Park Service, Jeremy A. Sabloff, Professor of Anthropology at the University of Pittsburgh, and George E. Stuart, Staff Archaeologist of the National Geographic Society, for reviewing the text and illustrations in this book and for providing expert advice and guidance during its preparation. We would also like to thank the National Park Service, the individuals and organizations named or quoted in the text, and those cited here for their generous assistance: Anthony P. Andrews, Kenneth E. Apschnikat, Grieg Arnold, Joe Baca, Bradley K. Baker, Ira Bartfield, Jan R. Bell, Frances Berdan, Debra Bodner, Natasha Bonilla, Donald L. Brockington, Yvonne Burket, Kathleen Byrd, John B. Carlson, Jefferson Chapman, A. William Creutz, Aron Crowell, Bruce H. Dahlin, Elin Danien, Manuel Díaz Baños, Christian E. Downum, Vada Dunifer, Melvin L. Fowler, Manuel A. Galvan, Clarence N. Gorman, Gary R. Graves, William Gustin, John B. Henry III, Robert C. Heyder, Mike Jacobs, W. James Judge, Duane E. King, Richard A. Knecht, James and Mary Koons, John F. Kramer, W. Phillip Krebs, Edward B. Kurjack, Dennis Labatt, Edmund J. Ladd, Bud Ledoux, John K. Loleit, Jeffrey Mauger, Kim McLean, Daniel M. McPike, Walter F. Morris, Jr., Henry B. Nicholson, William H. Nolan, Martha Potter Otto, Maria Pascua, Gordon L. Pullar, Ann M. Renker, Everett Routzen, Gerald F. Schroedl, David G. Smith, Dean R. Snow, Vincas P. Steponaitis, Roberto Stuart, Thomas G. Vaughan, John A. Walthall, David Webster, Warren L. Wittry, Barton Wright.

For quotations from American Indian stories and poems, we gratefully acknowledge the following: **Pages 41, 44, and 49:** Richard Erdoes and Alfonso Ortiz, eds., *American Indian Myths and Legends* (New York: Pantheon Books, 1984), pp. 105-106. **Page 110:** Frank Hamilton Cushing, *Zuñi Folk Tales* (New York and London: G. P. Putnam's Sons, 1901), pp. 425 and 428. **Pages 177, 180, and 186:** Miguel León-Portilla, *Pre-Columbian Literatures of Mexico,* translated by Grace Lobanov and the Author (Norman and London: University of Oklahoma Press, 1986), pp. 81, 87, 91, and 95. **Page 180:** John Bierhorst, ed., *In the Trail of the Wind: American Indian Poems and Ritual Orations* (New York: Farrar, Straus and Giroux, 1971), p. 44.

ILLUSTRATIONS

We are indebted to the following museums and other institutions for permitting Rik Cooke to photograph artifacts in their collections and for providing pertinent information: The Louisiana Office of State Parks, The Carl Alexander Collection (18 upper left and right); Ohio Historical Society (23, 27, 29, 30); University of Alabama State Museum of Natural History (38 upper and lower); The Center for the Arts, Vero Beach, Florida, for artifacts on temporary loan from the Philbrook Art Center and from the Collections of The Thomas Gilcrease Institute of American History and Art, Tulsa, Oklahoma (41); Frank H. McClung Museum, The University of Tennessee (47); Museum of Indian Archaeology/London, Ontario, Canada (48, 51); Museum of the American Indian-Heye Foundation (49, 86); Makah Cultural and Research Center (60 upper, 63); National Museum of Natural History, Smithsonian Institution (65, 66); Kodiak Archaeological Project (67); Arizona State Museum, University of Arizona (81, 84, 85 upper and lower, 99); National Park Service Chaco Collection, University of New Mexico (90); Chaco Culture National Historical Park

(96); Mesa Verde National Park (102, 103); Jalapa Museum, Vera Cruz, Mexico (116, 117, 121); Museo Nacional de Antropología, Mexico City, Mexico (124, 171, 176, 187); Museo Regional de Copan, Instituto Hondureño de Antropología e Historia, and The Anthropology Museum, Northern Illinois University (151).

GRANT RECIPIENTS

Beginning with Hiram Bingham's explorations at Machu Picchu in 1912, the National Geographic Society has supported the work of scholars at archaeological sites around the world. We acknowledge with pleasure the contributions of all recipients of Society grants in archaeology, and we welcome this opportunity to list by grant year those who have worked at sites included in *America's Ancient Cities:* Neil M. Judd, Smithsonian Institution, Pueblo Bonito, 1920-29; Matthew W. Stirling, Smithsonian Institution, La Venta, 1938-47, '54; Philip Drucker, Smithsonian Institution, La Venta, 1942, '47; H. Douglas Osborne, National Park Service, Mesa Verde, 1958-63, '65; Eusebio Dávalos Hurtado, National Institute of Anthropology and History of Mexico, Chichen Itza, 1960-61; Robert F. Heizer, University of California, La Venta, 1967, '69; Jeremy A. Sabloff, Harvard University, Cozumel, 1971-73; Arthur G. Miller, Yale University, Tulum, 1972, '74; Thomas R. Lyons, New Mexico Archeological Center, National Park Service, Chaco Canyon, 1973; Dennis J. Stanford, Smithsonian Institution, Colorado mammoth kill sites, 1973-77; William R. Coe, University of Pennsylvania, Quirigua, 1974-75; William A. Longacre, University of Arizona, Grasshopper Pueblo, 1974; William J. Folan and George E. Stuart, National Geographic Society, Coba, 1974-75; Edward B. Kurjack, Western Illinois University, Pre-Columbian settlement patterns in Yucatan, 1975; Jefferson Chapman, University of Tennessee, Cherokee town sites in Tennessee, 1976; Robert J. Sharer, University of Pennsylvania, Quirigua, 1976-79; Mason E. Hale, Smithsonian Institution, Tikal, 1978-79; Ray T. Matheny, Brigham Young University, and Bruce H. Dahlin, Catholic University of America, El Mirador, 1979, 1981-82; Charles E. Lincoln, Peabody Museum, Harvard University, Chichen Itza, 1983; Dean R. Snow, State University of New York at Albany, Mohawk village sites in New York State, 1983, '85; William L. Fash, Jr., Northern Illinois University, Copan, 1986-87; Jonathan Haas, School of American Research, Tsegi Canyon rock-shelters, 1986.

Library of Congress CIP Data

Stuart, Gene S.
America's ancient cities / [by Gene S. Stuart; photographed by Richard Alexander Cooke III; paintings by H. Tom Hall]; prepared by the Special Publications Division, National Geographic Society, Washington, D.C.
   p.   cm.
Bibliography: p.
Includes index.
ISBN 0-87044-627-4 (regular edition)
ISBN 0-87044-632-0 (library edition)
1. Indians of North America—Antiquities. 2. Cities and towns, Ruined, extinct, etc.—North America. 3. Indians of Mexico—Antiquities. 4. Cities and towns, Ruined, extinct, etc.—Mexico. 5. Indians of Central America—Antiquities. 6. Cities and towns, Ruined, extinct, etc.—Central America. 7. North America—Antiquities. 8. Central America—Antiquities. 9. Mexico—Antiquities. I. National Geographic Society (U.S.). Special Publications Division. II. Title.
E77.9.S78 1988
970.01—dc 19   87-34851
                                                               CIP

Index

ADDITIONAL READING

The reader may wish to consult the *National Geographic Index* for related articles and books. The following may also prove useful: **GENERAL:** Michael D. Coe *et al., Atlas of Ancient America;* Kingsley Davis, ed., *Cities;* Franklin and Mary Elting Folsom, *America's Ancient Treasures;* W.H. Freeman, ed., *Cities;* Jesse D. Jennings, *Prehistory of North America;* David and Joan Oates, *The Rise of Civilization;* Richard Shutler, Jr., ed., *Early Man in the New World;* Ray A. Williamson, *Living the Sky.* **THE EASTERN WOODLANDS:** David S. Brose *et al., Ancient Art of the American Woodland Indians;* Jefferson Chapman, *Tellico Archaeology;* Charles Hudson, *The Southeastern Indians;* William N. Morgan, *Prehistoric Architecture in the Eastern United States;* Martha A. Potter, *Ohio's Prehistoric Peoples;* Robert Silverberg, *Mound Builders of Ancient America;* John A. Walthall, *Prehistoric Indians of the Southeast.* **THE PLAINS AND THE NORTHWEST:** Richard D. Daugherty and Ruth Kirk, *Hunters of the Whale;* Don E. Dumond, *The Eskimos and Aleuts;* John C. Ewers, *Indian Life on the Upper Missouri;* H.R. Hays, *Children of the Raven;* Jesse D. Jennings, ed., *Ancient North Americans;* Harold McCracken, *George Catlin and the Old Frontier;* Davis Thomas and Karin Ronnenefeldt, eds., *People of the First Man;* Reuben Gold Thwaites, ed., *Original Journals of the Lewis and Clark Expedition.* **THE SOUTHWEST:** J.J. Brody *et al., Mimbres Pottery;* Emil W. Haury, *The Hohokam;* Dewitt Jones and Linda S. Cordell, *Anasazi World;* Robert H. and Florence C. Lister, *Those Who Came Before;* David Grant Noble, *Ancient Ruins of the Southwest;* Clara Lee Tanner, *Prehistoric Southwestern Craft Arts.* **MESOAMERICA:** Michael D. Coe, *Mexico* and *The Maya;* Michael D. Coe and Richard A. Diehl, *In the Land of the Olmec;* Nigel Davies, *The Ancient Kingdoms of Mexico* and *The Aztecs;* Bernal Díaz del Castillo, *True History of the Conquest of New Spain;* Fray Diego Durán, *The Aztecs,* tr. and ed. Doris Heyden and Fernando Horcasitas; Jorge E. Hardoy, *Pre-Columbian Cities;* Doris Heyden and Luis Francisco Villaseñor, *The Great Temple and the Aztec Gods;* Joyce Kelly, *The Complete Visitor's Guide to Mesoamerican Ruins;* Miguel León-Portilla, *The Broken Spears;* Jaime Litvak King, *Ancient Mexico;* Mary Ellen Miller, *The Art of Mesoamerica from Olmec to Aztec;* A.R. Pagden, tr. and ed., *The Maya: Diego de Landa's Account of the Affairs of Yucatán* and *Hernán Cortés: Letters from Mexico;* Esther Pasztory, *Aztec Art;* Linda Schele and Mary Ellen Miller, *The Blood of Kings;* John Lloyd Stephens, *Incidents of Travel in Central America, Chiapas and Yucatán;* Muriel Porter Weaver, *The Aztecs, Maya, and Their Predecessors.*

Composition for *America's Ancient Cities* by the Typographic section of National Geographic Production Services, Pre-Press Division. Set in Palatino. Printed and bound by Holladay-Tyler Printing Corp., Rockville, Md. Film preparation by Catharine Cooke Studio, Inc., New York, N.Y. Color separations by Lanman Progressive Company, Washington, D.C.; Lincoln Graphics, Inc., Cherry Hill, N.J.; and NEC, Inc., Nashville, Tenn.